CADDIE CONFIDENTIAL

GREG "PIDDLER" MARTIN

TRIUMPH
BOOKS

No part of this publication may be reproduced, stored in a retrieval system, or transmitted in any form by any means, electronic, mechanical, photocopying, or otherwise, without the prior written permission of the publisher, Triumph Books, 542 South Dearborn Street, Suite 750, Chicago, Illinois 60605.

Triumph Books and colophon are registered trademarks of Random House, Inc.

Library of Congress Cataloging-in-Publication Data
Martin, Greg.
    Caddie confidential / Greg Martin.
        p. cm.
    Includes bibliographical references and index.
    ISBN 978-1-60078-190-2 (alk. paper)
    1. Caddies—Anecdotes—Anecdotes. 2. Golf—Tournaments
        I. Title.
GV970.M365 2009
796.352′66—dc22   2008045499

This book is available in quantity at special discounts for your group or organization. For further information, contact:

> **Triumph Books**
> 542 South Dearborn Street
> Suite 750
> Chicago, Illinois 60605
> (312) 939-3330
> Fax (312) 663-3557

Printed in U.S.A.
ISBN: 978-1-60078-190-2
Design by Sue Knopf
Photos courtesy of AP Images unless otherwise noted

To Mom, Dad, Kathleen,
and all caddies
living and dead

Contents

WHY IN THE WORLD DO WE NEED CADDIES?

People ask me all the time, "Who do you hang out with on Tour? Do you go out to dinner with Phil? With Tiger?" The truth is, most of my friends on Tour are caddies, and I can honestly say that I'd rather go to dinner with them than with players.

Caddies are an essential part of a pro's game and I love hanging out with them, but sometimes being good friends can be a hindrance on the course. It can even result in someone losing a job. The last caddie I had was a really good guy and I liked him a lot. In fact, I wanted to play well for him so much that it was hurting my game. I got to a point where I just wasn't making any putts. Instead of focusing on my game, I was wondering what he must be thinking. Day after day he watched me miss putts, costing him money with every bad shot.

I put enough pressure on myself—I don't need it from anywhere else. So, even though he had become one of my best friends, I had to fire him. Sure enough, once I hired someone who just wanted to go out there and have a good time, the pressure was off and I won the first tournament with him on my bag. Maybe I'm too sensitive, or maybe I like and respect my caddies too much. I have to remind myself (and my caddies) that getting fired is just another part of professional golf. It's usually more about superstition than it is about caddying ability. When you get in a rut and nothing is clicking, the first thing a player thinks about changing isn't his putter, it's his caddie. They're an indispensable part of the game, but they come and go like the wind.

—MARK CALCAVECCHIA

How much did my caddie mean to me? A lot. Maybe too much. He meant so much to me that I married him. And then divorced him.

—DOTTIE PEPPER

Like any service industry, a caddie's job is to anticipate and be one step ahead of what might be coming. It is easier said than done. There are times when you're under the pressure of a tournament and you're going down the stretch and the only thing that you need as a player is the trusted counsel of a confidant. Golfers pride themselves on being focused and independent, but we can't be too independent. We need feedback.

Caddies also need to be focused. Because I am a veteran player I am usually paired with other veteran players who often have longtime caddies by their side. It can seem like one big happy family out there, but it's not. It's very competitive and you need to realize the magnitude of the challenge you're facing. Golf is a psychological game. Both you and your caddie have to use every ounce of your mental and physical capacities to gain some advantage and to do well. There are little things that a caddie can say or suggest to a player at just the right time. Sometimes you will listen and other times you might be too stubborn to consider what your caddie has to offer, but over time you build a relationship with your caddie based on trust, faith, and belief. A really good caddie possesses a high level of emotional intelligence and is able to communicate with you nonverbally. When you get to that level with your caddie you increase your potential for success.

These days, players look for every little edge they can get on the competition and the caddie can certainly make the difference. It wasn't always this way. Ten or 15 years ago, caddies were known for being very entertaining and quick with a story. They were quite a cast of characters. Now, because the stakes have gone up, it has become very competitive and tough for caddies to even get a job. Players are forming partnerships with their caddies to help them get to the top. It's no longer just working up the ropes. It's preparation before the tournament, caddying well and with unwavering focus, and follow-up reviews at the end of the day. It has certainly evolved.

Greg and I have had one of the longest working relationships on Tour and I share with him a lot of great memories. Like any relationship, we've had our ups and downs. There is one mishap that Greg will probably never be able to forget. I know I won't. It was a Saturday in 2002 at Bay Hill, and at the time I was tied for seventh place. We were on the 18th green. Greg was helping Brett Quigley (who was paired with us) with his drop near the bunker. On his first drop the ball rolled in the bunker and Greg raked it out for him. The second drop was clearly going to roll in the bunker again, and Greg stopped the ball before it went in. According to the rulebook, the ball must come to a complete stop before you can pick it up, but not one of us realized anything illegal had just transpired. We finished our putts, shook hands, signed our cards, and headed across the street. While we were signing some autographs a spectator with a heavy German accent said to me, "I thought you guys played by the rules here!" I told him we did and suggested that if he saw an infraction he should contact an official. It was an unfortunate suggestion, because he went and did exactly that. Both Greg and I felt pretty good about my chances to win the tournament. I was playing well and in the hunt going into final day. Then, on my drive to the course on Sunday morning, I heard on the local sports radio station that Brett Quigley had been disqualified from the tournament because of the way his drop had been handled. To make things worse, I had also been disqualified because it was my caddie who picked up the ball before it stopped.

A similar thing happened to Mark O'Meara and his caddie at the San Diego Open around the same time. Mark took a drop and his ball started rolling down the cart path. His caddie picked it up before it came to a stop. An official came running out and explained that this was an infraction, but the rule states that if the pick-up occurs outside two club lengths of the drop then it's not a penalty. They took out Mark's putter, his shortest club (the rule doesn't specify which club), and measured. No penalty was assessed. If we'd known that, our infraction may well have been outside two putter lengths, and Quigley and I would not have been disqualified. You live and you learn. Suffice it to say, Greg made a little history that day by getting two players thrown out of a PGA Tournament on a Saturday.

—DAN FORSMAN

WHY CADDIES ARE
SO DAMN GREAT

Nobody knows the game of golf like a caddie. The caddie sees it all: the unrelenting dreams, jaw-dropping victories, and soul-crushing defeats. They rarely receive credit when things go right and frequently take the blame when things go wrong, yet they are the invisible backbone of the game. Behind every top-10 finish, every Tour championship, and every missed cut there is a guy pulling clubs for his pro. For decades, these "loopers" were viewed as second-class citizens, often staying five or more to a room in dive motels. It was a job for alcoholics, drug addicts, and high-school dropouts. In the '80s, as tournament purses started to increase dramatically, a skilled and reliable caddie became invaluable to a golfer's success. Today the caddie's lifestyle can consist of private jets, tournaments in exotic beachside locales, and, perhaps most importantly, getting one's own bed on the road. When a six-figure payday rests on the swing of the proper club, a high-caliber caddie is essential.

He is part-time meteorologist, part-time mathematician, and full-time therapist. He will deftly predict wind conditions;

ensure that a superstitious player always has his lucky penny, nickel, or dime in his pocket before hitting the links; reserve unlucky No. 4 balls for pro-ams only; understand how the grass condition and growth pattern on a course will affect every shot; and pull the right iron on a million-dollar hole. Put simply, the Tour caddie's knowledge of the game is unsurpassed.

Gleaned from many, many interviews with my caddie buddies on the PGA circuit, this book is an unprecedented look at the game. Anecdotes, practical tips, superstitions, and infamous stories that have until now been told only in our inner circle fill these pages, making *Caddie Confidential* the most comprehensive collection of golf tales and advice ever assembled by the unsung heroes of the game. Read it, play well, and don't forget to tip your caddie.

The Unusual Suspects (and Their Players)

- Greg "Piddler" Martin (Mark Calcavecchia, Dan Forsman)
- Al Melan (Steve Pate, Jeff Sluman)
- "Alaskan" Dave Patterson (Craig Stadler, Joe Daley)
- Anthony Wilds (David Peoples)
- Artie Granfield (Byron Nelson, J.C. Snead)
- Bill "Junkman" Jenkins (Allison Finney)
- Billy Carlucci (Jeff Brehaut)
- Bob "Mr. Clean" Chaney (Scott McCarron, Bart Bryant)
- Brian Lietzke (Bruce Lietzke)
- Chip "Alabama" Carpenter (Chris Riley)
- Chris "Crispy" Jones (Mark Wilson)
- Chuck Hart (executive advisor of the Professional Tour Caddies Association)
- Chuck Mohr (Bob Estes, Mike Reid)
- Dale McElyea (Steve Lowery)
- Dave "Reptile" Lemon (John Daly, Vijay Singh)

- Dick "the Angel" Martin (Juli Inkster, Mike Donald, John Morris)

- Donna Earley (Jennifer Rosales, Nancy Lopez)

- Eric Schwarz (Corey Pavin, Fuzzy Zoeller)

- Fred Burns (Hal Sutton)

- Graeme Courts (Loren Roberts, Ian Leggatt, Brad Faxon)

- Hilton "J.J." James (Isao Aoki, Steve Pate)

- Jeff "Boo" Burrell (Billy Ray Brown)

- Jeff Dolf (Craig Stadler)

- Jeff Kaleita (Gavin Coles)

- Jeff "the Shadow" Jones (Soo Young Moon)

- Jeff "Skillet" Willet (Brian Bateman)

- Richard "Jelly" Hansberry (Tim Petrovic)

- Jerry "Speedway" Aiken (Sam Snead)

- Jerry "Skyscraper" Schneider (Betsy King, Woody Blackburn)

- Jim "Springboard" Springer (Bill Glasson, Gene Sauers, David Peoples)

- Jim "Bones" Mackay (Ernie Els, Phil Mickelson)

- Joe "Freak" Bosowski (Hal Underwood)

- Joe LaCava (Fred Couples)

- Joey Damiano (Stuart Appleby)

- John "Cadillac" Carpenter (J.P. Hayes, Fuzzy Zoeller)

The Unusual Suspects (and Their Players)

- John "Chief" Griffin (Blaine McCallister, Tom Byrum)

- John Buchna (Joey Sindelar)

- John "Doc" Roman, Tour Chiropractor

- Kenny Butler (David Toms)

- Linn "the Growler" Strickler (Curtis Strange, Ben Crenshaw, Fred Couples, Payne Stewart)

- Mark Chaney (Jeff Sluman, Curtis Strange, Steve Flesch)

- "Minnesota" Mike Lealos (T.C. Chen, Bill Glasson)

- "Reefer" Ray Reavis (Ben Bates)

- Richard Motacki (Tommy Armour III)

- Rick "Rick at Nite" Hippenstiel (Don Pooley)

- Rocky Hobday (Mark James)

- Tom Anderson (Tommy Armour III, David Frost, Carl Pettersson, John Cook)

- Tom Janis (Paul Azinger, Mark O'Meara)

- Tom Thorpe (Nancy Lopez, Lorena Ochoa)

ONE

THE ART OF CADDYING

CADDIE CREDO #1:
Show up, shut up, and keep up.

Caddying is the best-kept secret in the world—it really is. I always tell people that if they're not coordinated or talented or lucky enough to be a professional athlete, caddying is the next best thing. When you go to the 18th hole of Augusta, the only people that can be on that green are the player and the caddie. It's one of the greatest thrills that you can have. It doesn't matter who you are—Tiger Woods, John Daly, or Dan Forsman. When a player has a one-shot lead with two holes to go, the only one who's rooting for him and really cares about him is his caddie. Of course, his wife is supporting him, but she's on the other side of the ropes. The caddie is the only one who is right there with him when it counts. And the pros know it. They listen to their caddies. It is a great job that a lot of people would pay to do. If there were an auction on eBay for the opportunity to caddie in the Masters, I bet people would pay a hundred grand for that privilege. We *get* paid to do it.

The job is so great that a caddie needs to do everything he can to protect it. That is why the first rule of caddying is this: If you can't make it to a tournament, find a replacement who is crummier than you. If your player says he doesn't want a smoker, get him a smoker. If he says he doesn't want anybody smelling like booze, get the drunkest guy you see in the bar that night. Once you have the job, it's yours until someone takes it away from you.

You also need a good work ethic. You have to be there, and be there on time. You have to get the wife to like you. You have to kiss the baby and say, "What a cute kid." If your player says he has another guy that week, you watch a couple holes to show him that you are interested. Everybody will tell you that you're a kissass, but you'll do anything to get and keep your job because it's the best gig in the world.

"The most valuable thing a caddie can do is to go after the guys with the nicest cars. I was working the Nike Tour. I was in the lot in Raleigh, North Carolina, and this guy drove up in a Toyota 4Runner. I thought, 'Man, he must play pretty well if he's got a brand new car like that.' I had no idea who he was but I asked him if he needed a caddie and he said he did. His name was Jeff Marlowe and I'll be damned if we didn't almost win that weekend. I finished out the whole year with him."

—JEFF KALEITA

"I've been lucky to get on with some great players and even luckier to be able to stay on those bags for a long time. What I've learned over the years is simple: success leads to longevity. I was with Ben Crenshaw for over 10 great years and he knew how to win with me on his bag. No matter what kind of pressure we were under, I was always laid back or if I wasn't, I would always do my best to appear to be cool, calm, and collected.

"The second-most important thing is to have a good sense of humor. After parting ways with Crenshaw I hooked up with Fred Couples. The only reason we worked so well together was that I could make him laugh. Fred can sometimes get too serious out on the golf course—you can see right away when he's feeling the pressure. Joking around distracted him from all the stress around him. I am convinced that it helped his game."

—LINN "THE GROWLER" STRICKLER

Can you pull the right club when you're under the gun? As a caddie, you're basically doing everything the player is doing except pulling the trigger—which is why I'd rather be a caddie than a player. You also need to know some key terms because when your player asks what he's doing wrong you need to have an answer—even if you don't have the slightest idea. These guys are so good that it's impossible to tell what, if anything, is wrong. You would need slow-motion video replay to accurately break down their swings, but you still need to say something because that's what you're getting paid to do. The answer I like best is *rhythm*. 'I think your rhythm is a little off' is always a good answer. *Tempo* also works. Give either one a try and you'll look like you know what you're talking about."

—JEFF "SKILLET" WILLET

Sensitive caddies don't last."

—BILL "JUNKMAN" JENKINS

I love the purity of the sport. If you can play well enough and get your score lower than anybody else you can win tournaments. And if you win some tournaments you can get in the Masters. And if you win that, you're big time. It could happen to anybody. It's so much better than signing a $10 million guaranteed contract just because you're a branded superstar. In golf, you can become a superstar by putting together a couple of good weeks.

"As for caddying, if you look at it in the big picture, it's just another form of gambling. But it's even better because you are right in the middle of the event. When you're on that stage supporting your player and hoping he hits the big time there, you have to be 100 percent in every moment of the tournament, be accurate with your numbers, and hopefully your instincts are right when you're guessing. I don't care what anybody says, when you're standing out there and the wind is howling and you're freezing your ass off, you're just guessing. 'I'm guessing you can get a five iron somewhere near the green.'"

—ANTHONY WILDS

I wash another man's balls for a living."
—"REEFER" RAY REAVIS

How could you have a better job in the world? You're on center stage in front of millions of people, you're inside the ropes, a part of the action. You actually have a say in what is going on, it's not that hard of work, and there's a bunch of money to be made."

—TOM JANIS

My advice to any caddie is to communicate with your player. I got Dicky Pride's bag for the Monday qualifier of the Reno/Tahoe Open in 2002. I got him through and helped him qualify for the tournament and was under the impression that I had the job for the tournament. After the round on Monday he told me he was using someone else. Never assume the job is yours!"

—CHRIS "CRISPY" JONES

Dan and me in the very early years (Photo courtesy of the author)

It's like you're playing a non-stop lottery. You can go from welfare to a Cadillac every week."
—DICK "THE ANGEL" MARTIN

A good caddie adapts to and reads his player's personality. For all caddies, the first thing is you have to show up on time. Just show up. It's not that hard. After that, almost every caddie on Tour is good at doing yardages, pulling clubs, reading greens, or whatever is asked by the player. But the most important thing is reading your player's personality and being whatever your player needs you to be: part-time psychologist or even full-time coach. You have to be able to read situations and know when to scream and shout or when to say something positive. I think a good caddie is not afraid to put himself out there on any given day. When you think it's time to say something, you've got to say it, even if that something might not want to be heard and could cause you to lose your job. A good caddie will speak his mind even though his head might be on the chopping block.

"Also, a caddie must always keep wind direction in the front of his mind. The wind can seriously mess up your player's shots. The first thing I do in the morning is grab the remote control and turn on the Weather Channel. Before news, before sports highlights, even before I eat, I find out which way the wind is blowing. Other than that, nothing else about weather interests me. If it rains, it rains. If it's sunny, it's sunny. Wind is the only thing that affects me as a caddie being able to pull the right clubs. Throwing a few blades of grass up in the air isn't going to tell me there is an east-northeast blowing at 10:00 AM and it will be switching to a northwest by 3:00 PM. I'm good, but I'm not that good. The Weather Channel has made my job much easier."

—AL MELAN

I love being outside and **caddying is a lot better than working for a living.** The worst thing about being a caddie is the travel, but it's also the best thing. The destinations more than make up for the journeys. For two weeks in January we're in Hawaii, then Florida for a couple weeks, followed by California for two weeks, then Puerto Vallarta for a week. It doesn't get much better than that. I work 22 weeks out of the year and that's it. A player just wants his caddie to show up, keep up, and shut up. That is all he wants. I have never, to this day, seen a caddie hit a shot for the player, but there are players out there who want their caddie to pull every club. Then, if things don't go well, they have somebody to blame.

"All Bruce has ever wanted me to do is be at the course an hour ahead of time and we call it a day as soon as he putts out. Now some 30-odd years into it, Bruce has made things a little easier for me: I only have to be at the course 45 minutes ahead of time. Thirty years has earned me 15 precious minutes."

—BRIAN LIETZKE

I think it's impossible to find a tighter group of guys. The caddies stick together. They'll bend over backwards for each other. Once I was stuck out at a tournament in Palm Springs with car trouble. A caddie who didn't have a job spent two days dealing with mechanics of questionable honesty and managed to get my car fixed and save me $800. He was between jobs and had the time off. I'm sure he didn't want to spend it at the garage but that's just what he did.

"Another time I was on a plane to Las Vegas when I met a caddie named Grady. We got to talking, and before I knew it, he gave me his job for the week. He was caddying for an amateur and didn't have another job lined up but was confident he could get another bag. It ended up being an over $1,000-per-week job when I was just getting started and really needed the money. He just did it out of the goodness of his heart. I've heard that he's done it for other guys too. Caddies are some of the highest-quality guys I've ever met. I can't say enough nice things about them. A lot of the pros don't treat us with the respect that we deserve. We take a lot of shit and we have to bite our tongues since our jobs are on the line. It can be hard. Unless you miss the cut, you really don't have days off, and most caddies would rather be in the hunt on the weekend than relaxing on the couch at home. As soon as the tournament is over on Sunday, we have got to hit the road and get to the next course by Monday. **It's not easy out here but we love it just the same.**"

—JOHN "DOC" ROMAN

Caddies are the greatest partiers in the world. One pro player started hanging out with us caddies and liked it so much he became one of us. He eventually earned the nickname 'Last Call' Lance. Also, you better like barbecues. We eat pretty much every meal off the grill 29 days a month."

—BILL "JUNKMAN" JENKINS

I always wanted to work outside, so my options were either landscaping or looping. I wasn't that good at pruning shrubbery, so I picked up a bag."

—RICHARD MOTACKI

You have about 10 jobs rolled into one. You have to give yardages. You have to read greens. You have to pull clubs. You have to be a sports psychologist. You have to control the crowd. It's a different kind of job that takes a different kind of person. You work half-days and half-years.

"When I was single, I loved my job more than anything. I still love my job, but I have a wife and two kids now. I've been in situations working for guys in a slump; the way they work out of it is by playing, playing, and then playing some more. To break the slump you might be on the road nonstop. And during a slump you're barely making enough money to get by. You're certainly not putting anything away in your kid's college fund."

—TOM ANDERSON

"My own golf game was pathetic. I had planned to do the caddie thing once, for something to do. That was about 20 years ago. I fell in love with it immediately. It was a way for me to be around the game without ever having to practice."

—DONNA EARLEY

"I learned this valuable lesson when I was caddying for Billy Ray Brown: You should always stick up for and take care of your player. Billy Ray was going through a bit of a rough patch, so whenever his score got worse than nine over, I'd tell the kid holding the scoreboard not to put any more numbers up there because it was getting a little demoralizing. Billy Ray liked that move so much that he told the other caddies in our group, 'Boo's the best caddie out here. He's much better than you and the others. You want to know why? It's because he knows enough to keep my scores off that scoreboard. That's exactly what my game needs.'"

—JEFF "BOO" BURRELL

"It's not that easy to get a good player. Actually, the whole job isn't that easy. It's a lot of hours spent just waiting around looking at your watch. Your player might tell you they're going in for a quick lunch and saunter back a couple of hours later. In the meantime, you've been waiting at the range in the hot sun with nothing to do. My advice would be to start caddying when you're young and you don't know any better."

—DONNA EARLEY

"Most players are Hour Guys: caddies have to be there an hour before tee time to warm up and then stay an hour after the round to work on a few things. I was someone who had it figured out down to the minute. It was like a game for me—how far was it and how long would it take me to get from my hotel to the range, always factoring in traffic issues. I was young and foolish—because showing up late has always been the number one reason for caddies to get fired. Nowadays I don't like to rush as much. I try to be there an hour-and-a-half before so I can have some breakfast and not just jump right into the round. These days I don't do a lot as far as preparation, because I've been out there so long that I already know most of the courses pretty well and I know that I'll be out there for the practice round and the pro-am to refamiliarize myself and check out any changes that have been made since playing it the year before.

—AL MELAN

"The best way to be a caddie is to be related to a player. You'll (almost) never get fired."

—"MINNESOTA" MIKE LEALOS

"If you want to be a caddie on Tour, don't be afraid to be wrong. That's one of the great things about the guy I work for now. 99 percent of the time I'm not wrong, but he allows me to be wrong. If I make a mistake, I'm not walking on eggshells. I don't have to become a yes-man to keep my job or stay out of trouble. You can't play scared—and you can't caddie scared either.

—TOM ANDERSON

" **Tiger calls it a sport, but it is really just a game— the greatest game of all.** It's forever changing and you can never conquer it. The caddie is there to perform his service and hopefully be a little bit of a good luck charm."

—JERRY "SPEEDWAY" AIKIN

" I love it. I'm living the dream. I love it because I make money at it, but it's not just the money. I can't imagine doing anything else. Of course, it's the hardest thing in the world to do if you're not making money, but it's the best thing to do if you are. A lot of guys are very good at what they do but they can't get work. It's a horrible life for them, paying out of their own pockets all the time. But even when I was down to my last $50 I still loved it. I never even thought of quitting. I knew something good would happen and it did—Stuart Appleby hired me.

"When I'm on the Tour, I'm an overpaid, underachieving babysitter. That's what I am. That's what we all are. I get out there and try my best to lead my player in the right direction.

"I am in a really great situation now because I am one of the few guys who Stuart listens to. He actually takes my opinion into consideration, even if we don't agree on things all the time. Like any job, there are some difficult moments.

"The hardest thing about caddying is keeping your player up when he's down and having the mental capacity to not show too much emotion, no matter if you're winning or you're losing. Of course, it's especially brutal when your guy is playing poorly. You try to do everything you can to help him, and if nothing works, then you start to fear for your job. But when your guy is playing well, life is great! All I do is stand next to him, make sure I'm handing him the right clubs, and stay out of his way. When he's playing badly, I have to try to keep him even. Stuart

11

and I don't disagree a lot, but we discuss a lot. Right, wrong, or indifferent I let him do what he wants to do. I put my two cents in, but I'll never overextend or tell him that he can't do something. I respect him too much for that."

—JOEY DAMIANO

It feels like I've been in college for the last 23 years, going out with friends and having a good time every week. If this isn't the best job in the world I don't know what is."

—TOM THORPE

I can't say that I absolutely love my job. When I started I really did get a kick out of it. Of course, I was only 18, so I didn't know any better. Back then, traveling all over America was exciting. We weren't playing for any real money so there was a lot more camaraderie back in the day. Now it's a lot more cutthroat than it used to be. The purses have gone up and there's a lot more at stake. You have people caddying out here from all different areas, all different lifestyles. You have people caddying out here that used to be stockbrokers. With a little bit of luck, you can make a really good living out here. It certainly isn't the way it used to be. Players will bring out friends and family to caddie for them now. It can hurt a golfer when he picks his unemployed brother-in-law who doesn't have the first clue about carrying a bag.

"The closeness that caddies used to share is long gone. But every now and then when a rain delay brings us all together, the stories start to flow and we still have a good laugh."

—MARK CHANEY

Most sports have a coach or a manager—somebody to blame when things go wrong, somebody who can call a time-out and make a speech or fine-tune something that can turn things around. Not golf. All the player has is his caddie, so you better know everything that your player needs or else you'll be the one taking the blame."

—"ALASKAN" DAVE PATTERSON

You're only as good as your player. You need to know what to say at the right time. Sometimes that means going an hour without talking. Other times you need to be talking about the women in the gallery or about last night's baseball scores. Knowing when to open your mouth and controlling what comes out of it is what makes a great caddie.

— JEFF "SKILLET" WILLET

I'm an old-school guy. I used to make fun of the guys who used the lasers for yardage but now I've come to realize that it really is helpful for me to get all my numbers. I also make fun of the caddies who wear two straps to carry the bag. Come on, man! It isn't a school backpack. Get rid of the second strap. I may have a bad back someday and regret poking fun at those guys, but for now I'm staying with the traditional single-strap bag."

—JOE LaCAVA

You need to have patience. There's a heck of a lot of waiting around in pro golf."

—DAVE "REPTILE" LEMON

" I love being in the action. You can't beat the nervous energy you get coming down the stretch in the final group on Sunday. And let's be honest, getting your face on network TV on Saturday and Sunday afternoons is pretty hard to beat.

—CHRIS "CRISPY" JONES

" How can it get any better than being able to make lots of money by being part of a game?"

—JIM "SPRINGBOARD" SPRINGER

" There are a lot of requirements for a good caddie. Probably the most important is that the caddie needs to be part-psychologist. I'd say to be successful, they have to be 50 percent psychologist. The emotional strain in that professional relationship can get really tough. They have to be able to deal with that. They have to know their man and who they're caddying for. They have to recognize when to speak up and when not to speak up, when to be encouraging and when to be pushy. It's a delicate balance.

"I think they need to have a pretty sophisticated understanding of the game. They're out there helping a guy pick clubs and the players are so good and consistent now that caddies should know exactly what club to pull for their pro before the pro knows himself. Caddies also need to understand wind and turf conditions, when the ball is going to spin, when it isn't going to spin, and when it's going to jump. They need to have an excellent understanding of the game because if they don't, they will get called out really fast. You can't fake it out there. The latest trend is that most caddies are former players, not just weekend warriors. These guys are serious players who truly know the game of golf.

On top of all this, it takes a certain personality to last out there, to be able to get along with your guy.

"The duties can go beyond just holding onto the bag; there are some valet responsibilities, too. There's some errand running. ('Get my clothes to the dry cleaner, get this to the laundry.') The pro's schedule can be so hectic that it is tough to keep up. A caddie has to be there for his player no matter what."

—CHUCK HART

Keep things positive! Let's say my player makes a swing and I don't think the tempo was very good. I'll say, 'Good tempo.' What that does is get him thinking about his tempo in a positive way. Also, never forget that you don't belong in every conversation.

"Make sure you provide perspective. I was working for Bart Bryant when he won the tournament at Memorial in 2005. Bart had just birdied 14 and we were standing on the 15th fairway. The field was down to just Freddie (Couples) and us, and Freddie was in the group right behind us. Bart was standing in the fairway waiting to hit his second shot after a perfect drive when all of a sudden we heard a big roar coming from the 14th green. Bart looked at me and said, 'Well, you don't have to turn around and look at the scoreboard to know what happened there.' I said, 'Yeah, he just made the exact same score you did. Big deal!' Bart just smiled, shook his head, and continued on to win the tournament."

—BOB "MR. CLEAN" CHENEY

My job isn't necessarily putting the right club in my pro's hands. My job has always been, in my mind, to make sure we don't brain cramp, to make sure that when he goes, '172. That's a 6 iron right?' I go, 'Yeah, right, 6 iron.'"

—AL MELAN

" I love my job to death. I'm a competitor. Hal (Sutton) has made me a competitor. I love golf, so I love getting up every morning to do my job. Even though we haven't played much lately, every morning when I get up I still know that this is my job. I get paid every week for doing this, whether we're on the golf course or not. I'm with him every time he picks up a golf club—at home or on the road—and I couldn't be happier about it."

—FRED BURNS

" If you really want to be a caddie, go to the Nationwide Tour and learn how to caddie properly. That's Caddying 101. There are systems in place—where to stand, when to walk, how to rake the bunker. Latch on to a young guy, then try to figure out who the good players are and work for them. You'll know the good players by the way they carry themselves. A good player should have a presence, a calm confidence."

—"MINNESOTA" MIKE LEALOS

" You need to be a man and stand up for yourself. **I don't think you're a good caddie unless you've been fired.**"

—DICK "THE ANGEL" MARTIN

" You need to know everything about that golf course. You need to know where the trouble is and how far it is from x to y. That's what the player wants from his caddie."

—BRIAN LIETZKE

" You've got to stand up for your man. I remember Steve (Lowery) had just made a bogey on the 18th up in Canada on a Saturday. As we were walking off the course, one of the marshals said to me, 'Your man's not playing so good, huh?' and I snapped back, 'No, the ones not playing so good left yesterday.'"

—DALE MCELYEA

Make sure that you never quit on your player. And I always make sure I get my check at the end of the week before I cuss him out."

—HILTON "J.J." JAMES

No matter who you are working for, you need to keep the basic stuff in mind. For example, it is really important to make sure your player is hitting the right ball. Mistakes happen way too often. My buddy Piddler had his player, Dan Forsman, hit the wrong ball on a Sunday afternoon for four holes once. It didn't end well."

—DICK "THE ANGEL" MARTIN

Try to stay positive and don't wear your emotions on your sleeve. Your player will easily pick up on any negative energy or stress and it certainly won't help their game. It's a little different being a caddie on the Ladies Tour. The women are so much more emotional and they need a lot more encouragement. They rely on their caddie much more than they do on the men's tour. I don't know if that's a good or bad thing."

—DONNA EARLEY

Approach the job like it's a real job, not like it's a game—even if it feels like a game and you're having a lot of fun. A caddie has to know his place. The more you are in your zone, the more you make your player feel like he doesn't have to worry about you, because you're on top of everything. If he feels like you're focused, he knows you can catch him if he's about to make a mistake. If he pulls a 4 iron out and you think it's too much club, he'll value your opinion. He may still hit it, but at least he'll think about it. Two brains are better than one—I guarantee you that."

—FRED BURNS

A lot in caddying depends on who you're working for. Obviously, getting the yardages correct is very important, but I think **it is just as important to know when to say something and when not to say something to a player.** You can certainly say the wrong thing and that does not help. Sometimes less is more. You just have to know what to say at the right time. That's something that can't be taught. It's instinct. If your personalities are reasonably compatible, I think you'll know what to say at the right time."

—MARK CHANEY

Work for somebody good, that way you'll make a lot of money."

—"MINNESOTA" MIKE LEALOS

I used to think that being a good caddie meant knowing the game and knowing the golf course, but I've come to learn that the most important thing is being able to relieve stress on the golf course. That can happen in a lot of different ways, but I've learned that the best way to relieve stress is by being confident. Your player will sense that confidence and play better. If something unexpected comes up, you just take it in stride and move on to the next shot."

—JOHN "CADILLAC" CARPENTER

Joe LaCava has caddied with Freddie Couples for as long as I can remember.

Always give your player plenty of club over water. There is nothing worse than hitting it short of the green and getting your ball wet. Also, never, ever over-caddie. Less is more, so stop yourself from falling into the old paralysis-through-analysis trap. Your player doesn't need a whole bunch of information running through his brain while he's trying to make his shots."

—"REEFER" RAY REAVIS

The one thing I'd tell a young caddie is **'Show up, shut up, and keep up.'** That applies to any job. *Show up* means making sure you're on time. *Shut up* doesn't mean you can't open your mouth—just don't put your foot in it. Saying the wrong thing at the wrong time can be worse than giving your player the wrong club. *Keep up* means being there ahead of your pro, with the yardage book in hand, already knowing which way the wind is blowing and having a mental list of the rundown for club selection on various holes. A player will always ask you things like that."

—RICK "RICK AT NITE" HIPPENSTIEL

You need to have a personality—but be careful not to have too much personality."

—ARTIE GRANFIELD

You need to have the answers to all of your player's questions, whether it be how far it is over the bunker, how far it is to the water, or where the pin is placed. You need to know these answers exactly, confidently, and definitively. You also need to know how your man is feeling, whether he wants to hit a hard shot or if he wants to hit a little soft cut."

—GRAEME COURTS

I've always lived by the motto that scared dogs don't hunt. It was for that reason I quit a player who I didn't think had what it took. Two years later that player was the leading money-winner on tour. I guess I should find a new motto."

—BILL "JUNKMAN" JENKINS

"   Half of the battle of being a caddie is getting along with the guy you are working for because you are going to be spending more time with him than you would your girlfriend or your wife. Also, it's always a good idea to walk the golf course before the tournament. Some guys give me a hard time about it. For example, I'll walk the L.A. Open course, even though I know it like the back of my hand. I've caddied it the last 15 years in a row and Fred (Couples) always plays well there, but I still like to do it because if I don't I will feel unprepared when we get to that first tee. I want to know exactly where that new bunker is and how it looks. When you walk the course, you can really get a feel for how the course is playing—if it's hard and fast, where the rough is, where the bad rough is, etc. It's well worth the walk."

—JOE LaCAVA

"   The best advice I can give to a young caddie is to not start at all. You have to remember that a full field in the summer has only 156 guys. I'm not saying that you can't be lucky and you shouldn't put your nuts out on the table to get whacked, but you have to know it's not easy to get a job. And you have to be able to take a lot of shit. Things will always go wrong. Everything is going to happen out on the course. Somebody's going to take a picture and the flash will get in your player's eyes, or the click from the camera will mess him up. Expect anything to happen. If you're caddying really well, nobody will even know you're there. People tend to notice you only if you make a mistake. Also, keep in mind that you're supplying the rhythm to your player—everything from the delivery of the club to the timing of the return of the ball."

—ANTHONY WILDS

"Younger caddies give me a whole bunch of respect for all the years I toiled on the Tour before they ever got here, which is great, but they sure as hell aren't going to help me find a job out here. It's not easy to survive as a Tour caddie. Jobs are hard to come by, and it's getting tougher every day. **That's why the best piece of advice is to find a good young up-and-coming player with a sister. Marry her and you'll have a job for life.**"

—LINN "THE GROWLER" STRICKLER

Two

Landing Your First Bag...
and Losing It

Caddie Credo #2:
*All that matters is that you've been hired
one more time than you've been fired.*
(Rocky Hobday)

The year was 1982. I was a member of one of Tacoma, Washington's, two exclusive country clubs. (Don't ask me how.) My girlfriend at the time was a pretty good golfer and she wanted to play an LPGA event in Seattle. In order to qualify, she had to win the Washington State Amateur. As fate would have it (and with me on the bag), we won. I had never caddied before but I sure let everyone in the tournament think that I was a pro. I completely intimidated all the other golfers with my fake professionalism. I'd have to say it was worth at least five shots that week!

After that win, my girlfriend had the fever. She wanted to turn pro. That's all well and good, but to turn pro when you're a nobody you need one thing above all else: money. I had been working in the radio and television business, and I quit my job, went out and bought some video equipment, and went with her on the LPGA road to seek out our fortune. In order to pay her entry fees, I went to all the Tuesday night parties before the pro-ams and offered my services to the amateurs to record the event. I'd yell out, "Who's got Nancy Lopez? Who's got Beth Daniels?" and sure enough, they wanted it on tape. Unfortunately, my battery would only last for six holes, so I'd go out with an early group, hustle back to charge my battery, go out with another group, charge my battery again, then go out one last time with a late group on their final six holes. I had a nice little entrepreneurial gig going until all my equipment was stolen at a tournament in New Orleans. After that, I decided it was time for something new. My girlfriend didn't end up cutting it on the Tour but I was loving caddying for some of the other ladies.

I made my big move and headed over to the men's tour. My first tournament was in Tucson, Arizona. I was in the parking lot with a bunch of other caddies—the parking lot is where all the action is. As players walked by, I asked the other caddies, "What about that guy?" and "What kind of player is he?" Every time they'd give the same answer. "Nah, he's no good," or "Don't waste your time; he's a stiff." Who knows if they were bullshitting me or not. They probably were. After all, there are no friends in the parking lot when you're a caddie. You're the best of friends at the bars after the tournaments but in the parking lots, where everyone is hustling for a job, you can't count on a single one to have your back. You pretend to like each other but you're really all enemies when you're standing out there. Hiding behind trees, hanging out at the luggage rack at the airport—it can take a lot of sneaking around to get a job. Finally, this guy came walking toward me carrying a golf bag with "Calcavecchia" written on it. I had no idea who he was, but I asked him if he had a caddie and he said he'd get back to me. (That's what they all say.) Meanwhile, I kept approaching any golfer with a heartbeat. Later that day, Calcavecchia came out of the clubhouse and told me me I was in. That put me in a celebratory mood, so I went to the bar with some of the caddies that night. There I am sitting at the bar, excited about my first PGA bag, and they ask me who I'm working for. I puff out my chest, proud as can be, and say, "His name is Mark Calcacasheea." Oops. I got corrected pretty damn quickly. Some of the guys still remind me of how stupid I was over a quarter century ago.

The next day I hit the course with Mark and it was like the first day of school, I was so excited. It was a match-play event and we were pitted against T.C. Chen. Calcavecchia (I made sure to get it right from that day on) was playing great, and we were up seven strokes at the turn. I was beginning to loosen up and the conversation started flowing. We were talking about football and I told him how much I liked the Washington Huskies and how they were going to win easily that weekend. Mark was surprised by how certain I was of this fact, so he called his bookie and put $50 on the Huskies. I told him not to worry, that it would be the easiest money he'd ever make. Apparently, T.C. Chen wasn't too impressed with my ability to pick football winners. T.C. went on to win the next nine holes and win the match. To make matters worse, the Huskies lost too. So in my first PGA event my player not only lost in match play, but he also lost 50 bucks. That was it with him—for a while at least.

"I was busted, disgusted, and couldn't be trusted. I had gone flat broke in Las Vegas and couldn't possibly return home to face my father. I got a job as a beer delivery guy and one day when the Ladies Tour came through town, a few buddies and I begged the caddie-master for a job. We followed them to the next event. **I loved it so much I sent in my letter of resignation on a postcard.**"

—BILL "JUNKMAN" JENKINS

"When Hal Sutton was a high school senior in Louisiana he was well known around town. Some buddies told me he was playing at a tournament in Huntington Park, so I decided to check him out. There was one man out there watching the high school kids play. Hal was leading by three when he hit his shot to the right on the last hole. The ball ended up in the woods behind a tree with a tiny opening to the hole. While the other spectator and I were waiting on Hal to finish, we started talking about the shot. I said all Hal need to do was chip it out on the fairway, make his bogey, and go home. Hal tried the shot through the little opening—too risky of a move—and somehow still made bogey to win. He shouldn't have tried it, but he didn't know any better. Two days later I got a call from a Mr. Howard Sutton. It turns out that the guy watching the tournament was Hal's father. He asked me to come to his office. I told him I didn't have any transportation and he told me to take a taxi. When I got to his office, he had a two-door Ford Fairlane Sports Coupe with a 489 engine waiting for me. "It's yours," he said. "You'll need it to get to the high school every afternoon so you can work with Hal." He also gave me $1,000 and guaranteed me another $250 a week. I didn't know this guy from Adam. But he liked the way I saw Hal's game and thought I could help him reach his potential. The year was 1977 and we've been together ever since. And I'll never forget that car. It rode better than any car I've had."

—Fred Burns

When I was a kid, I caddied at the local country club so I could afford to buy my first car. Then I worked all the 'real' jobs—the steel mill, the meatpacking plants, all kinds of restaurants. One day I got laid off from a job, so with my newfound free time I headed to the golf course to hit some balls. Right when I got there I ran into Rick "Rick at Nite" Hippenstiel, who I'd caddied with as a kid. Rick had become the caddie-master at the country club. The next thing I knew I was doing a couple of loops for him. Winter rolled around and Rick was heading to California to do the West Coast swing. It sounded good to me so we split expenses and headed out there. He picked up two bags over six weeks. I didn't pick up any, but I worked the pro-ams and made some money to get by. But I didn't want to just get by. I was hungry to land a bag and to start making some money. So I decided it was time to get a little more aggressive. This was my new strategy for getting a bag, and I can't believe they didn't kick me out of parking lots for doing this: when a pro came out of the clubhouse and was going to the range, I literally bumped into him. He'd see my face, I'd say 'Good morning,' and when he came back I did the same thing. With 144 players, that's 288 bumps a day for six weeks. That's a lot of contact. Unfortunately it didn't work. All it really seemed to do was make players go out of their way to get around me so I wouldn't be able to bump them. My plan backfired and players began to ignore me. It was not the way to get a job.

"I went back home to Ohio and cried in my beer for a while. I figured that maybe I had tried too hard by trying to force myself onto a player, but I knew I could be a good caddie. So I bought a ticket down to New Orleans for a tournament and that was where I finally caught a break. Thomas Levet came over from France with an exemption. I'd never bumped into him…I was the first one he talked to and he hired me on the spot. That was the momentum I needed. In the next eight weeks I picked up seven different bags and things just fell into place from there."

—BOB "MR. CLEAN" CHANEY

I caddied in Akron, Ohio, at the American Golf Classic in 1976. Back then they didn't use Tour caddies. Instead, they had all of the 'potential caddies' pick numbers. We each grabbed a number and whatever preselected player the number corresponded to was who you got. It was kind of like a dating game. I was pretty lucky in picking numbers—one year I picked Jack Nicklaus. To be honest, that experience of looping for Jack got me hooked. **Like most veteran caddies, I hadn't planned to be out on Tour for all that long, but that was over 30 years ago, and I'm still here."**

—JEFF "BOO" BURRELL

A friend of mine that I played with on the mini tours, Stephen Gangluff, made it through all three stages of Q-School in 2002 with his wife as his caddie. He later called me to work for him the next year. I jumped at the opportunity and I haven't looked back since."

—JEFF "SKILLET" WILLET

My first bag was with Gary Koch at Riviera (Country Club) in Los Angeles. All I remember about that week is that we were paired with Jack Nicklaus on Thursday and Friday. It was

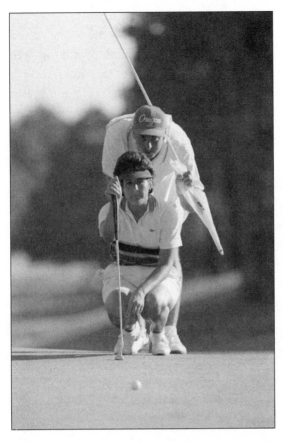

Tom Thorpe with Nancy Lopez, notching her 42nd win on the Ladies Tour

a pretty big thrill. On the first tee box you're up on a cliff with about a 75-foot drop. I was on such a high because it was my first bag and because we were with Jack. It was like a dream. I remember standing there in awe watching Jack get ready to hit his tee shot and I was slowly backing up, not paying attention to my surroundings, when suddenly Angelo (Argea, Nicklaus' longtime caddie) grabbed my arm and stopped me from falling off the cliff. **Another step and I'd have been gone."**

—RICHARD MOTACKI

"   I caddied for the Australian PGA at my home course when I was 14 years old. I was a junior at the club, and the head pro asked me if I was interested in caddying for him. I showed up at the golf course on Monday and worked for a guy by the name of Mike Cahill. We were paired with Wayne Riley who had just come off a great week at the British Open. Riley had an old Scotsman on the bag who he brought down with him from the European Tour. When we got to the 2nd hole Wayne Riley asked his caddie a question and all I remember is his caddie answering with all of these strange numbers and wind conditions. I didn't know anything about it. I just thought that a caddie's responsibility was to carry the bag. It really opened my eyes to how professional a caddie has to be. Strangely enough, we had a top-10 finish that week even though I had no idea what I was doing. It was clearly a case of beginner's luck."

—GRAEME COURTS

"   When you're out there, the average caddie can do a lot of struggling. Early on when I started on the Tour, I was caddying for a handful of people, jumping from bag to bag trying to make my way. At one point I was caddying for Matt Gogel and for some reason we split up. I came back to my hometown of Westchester, New York, to hang out with my parents for a couple of weeks. Then I drove down to an event in Philadelphia looking for some work. I wound up caddying for who I thought at the time was a decent player for the week. My guy really struggled and we missed the cut by something ridiculous—seven, eight, nine shots. After the round on Friday he said to me, "Hey, if you want to come down to Texas with me next week, you can. But if you don't want to, I understand—I'm not playing that well right now." I took him up on the offer and he played great. He played so well that we were in the last group with Justin Leonard on Sunday. We wound up finishing solo second and earning a great paycheck. That definitely made me want to keep caddying for as long as possible."

—BILLY CARLUCCI

I wouldn't trade my job as a caddie for anything. I remember working in broadcasting 30 years ago after college up in Washington State. It rained every f—ing day and all I wanted to do was be out on the golf course. After a couple months in Washington I got in my car and drove down to Palm Springs to get a bag. I have never, ever regretted it."

—ERIC SCHWARZ

The year was 1972. I had just turned 21 and I was fresh out of the service. I had a good buddy named Jim Barber who I went to high school with down in Clearwater, Florida. Jim was a great golfer and he'd turned pro a couple of years earlier. I had made a promise to myself to see the country and I thought, 'What better way to see it than to work my way across it as a caddie?' So I offered my services to Jim and he took me up on them. Things didn't really work out with him, but I managed to keep traveling around, working for anyone who would take me. Then from '73 to '77 I used the GI Bill to go to university, but it was too late—I already knew what I wanted to do and it certainly wasn't going to be a nine-to-five office job. **Working outside while being part of a major-league sport was unbeatable.** So I put all of that hard-earned education to good use by hitting the Tour and caddying full time."

—LINN "THE GROWLER" STRICKLER

"Just before the Nike Tour came to my hometown, there was a volunteer sign-up sheet in a local hotel lobby. I had the intention of going down there to sign up as a hole marshal. I heard they needed caddies so I thought, 'What the heck, it's better than a hole marshal. This way I can get inside the ropes and see what's really going on.' I signed up for it, got a bag, my guy made the cut, and I've been doing it for over a decade now."

—JEFF KALEITA

"The first pro I ever worked for was David Peoples—in 1984 at the Tucson Match Play. I got the job because I went out to the golf course and hung around the parking lot. Lucky for me, Peoples' caddie didn't show up so I jumped at the chance to work for him."

JIM "SPRINGBOARD" SPRINGER

"I grew up in Washington, DC, and lived right across from Langston Country Club. I didn't have much money and my grandmother couldn't afford to give me a dollar, so I'd just go across the street and caddie.

"My first pro bag was with Nate Starks in 1970, and I went on to work with Jim Thorpe for 10 years before he got to the PGA Tour. I was still working my regular job back then, so I would only caddie on weekends. I worked for the District government for 30 years and would use my vacation time to go to tournaments in the summer. After 1980, I figured I could make a steady income caddying and so I started doing it full time."

—RICHARD "JELLY" HANSBERRY

"Bob Gilder brought me out here. He's on the Senior Tour now. I was living in Los Angeles and working at a country club. A doctor who I caddied for was a friend of Gilder. Turns out Gilder was the first alternate in the Los Angeles Open that year, but he ended up not getting in the tournament, so he came out to our club that Thursday instead of playing at Riviera. I worked for him and on the 10th hole and asked him if he had a regular caddie. He said he didn't and asked, "Why, you want to come out?" I said, "Absolutely." The next week I came out and we finished third at a Nike Tour event. He told me he was going to spend most of the rest of the year on Tour and asked if I wanted to come work for him. Again, I said, "Absolutely." I was living at home with my father. I didn't have a family, didn't have a girlfriend. I didn't really leave anything behind, to be quite honest. I just went out on the road. I think I worked 15 weeks in a row—not just with Gilder, but with other guys as well. It took me about two weeks to pay my dues with the other caddies. **It wasn't until after a few really late nights at the local bars that I was completely accepted into the caddie world.**"

—Tom Anderson

"I never really planned to be a caddie, but the profession just kept drawing me in. I was backpacking across Europe trying to get a job here, there, or wherever just to make a little money to survive. I worked in some pubs in London for a while, eventually made my way down to Lisbon in search of some sunshine, and came across the Portuguese Open. I went down to the golf course, got a bag with an Australian pro and caught the caddie bug. But still, I wasn't planning on being a caddie. I already had a job in the printing business that allowed me to work for six months of the year and travel the other six. It was a pretty good deal for me and I wasn't looking for anything else.

"The next year I was backpacking across Canada when my good friend Steve Rintoul, who is now a rules official on the PGA Tour, asked me to caddie for him on the Canadian Tour. Not long afterward I hooked up with John Morse, who played really well and earned an exemption on the Australian Tour. I wasn't planning on continuing to caddie back in Australia. I was all set to return to my printing job, but John convinced me to stay with him. By Christmas I was ready to go back to my real job because John was playing so poorly that I wasn't making any money. The printing business was more reliable. But he convinced me to stay with him for one more tournament. After Christmas we went out to Perth and John finished third. The week after, at the Australian Masters, he finished second. (As always, Norman won that one.) After those two nice checks in a row I forgot about my 'real' job and stayed with him through the Asian Tour and again back through Canada, where John came in first on the money list. Then we went back to Australia and John won the Australian Open in my hometown of Sydney.

"A couple years later I'd had enough of caddying and I was all set to returning to my printing job. This time I was serious and I told everybody at work that I would see them on Monday morning. The week leading up to my return I picked up the bag for a young kid who just turned pro, Michael Campbell. We won the Canon Challenge in Sydney that weekend. It had to be a sign of some kind. **How could I possibly leave caddying and walk away from all this winning?**"

—GRAEME COURTS

" In the early 1970s I was living in Palm Springs where every year they hold the Bob Hope Classic. A friend of mine

34

qualified for the tournament as an amateur and I was going to caddie for him. Bruce Fleisher's caddie got into some kind of trouble and missed his tee time so Bruce asked me to work for him. My friend didn't really seem to mind so I took the offer. We did pretty well and he gave me a bunch of cash. I didn't even know they paid the caddies—I was just out there to have a good time. Then Bruce asked me to meet him in Phoenix for the next tournament. I didn't know we had to be there on Monday, so I showed up late, and lost the job with Fleisher. But I quickly found another bag and another paycheck."

—JOHN "CHIEF" GRIFFIN

My very first bag on tour was with Steve Pate. I did 17½ years with him, which was sort of unheard of during those years, and we became good friends, which was also sort of unheard of. The only reason we parted was that he was starting a third year without his card and I just wasn't able to make a living working with him anymore. I still stay in touch with him. We have plans to get together when he turns 50 and joins the Senior Tour. He was my first job on the PGA Tour and it lasted a very long time. It became more than just a working relationship and I am grateful for that."

—AL MELAN

I caddied as a kid and I was always around golf. For a few years, I was just working at clubs handling the bag room and whatever else was thrown my way. In '87, I caddied in a couple of events for the PGA Senior Tour. I came up to the northeast for the summer, hit Hartford and that was it. Bobby Clampett was my first pro bag. I got him in the parking lot in Hartford—I just walked up to him and asked him if he needed anybody. He didn't know me, I didn't know him. It was a

Tuesday morning. I was living in New Jersey, so I just drove up to Hartford and took a shot.

"Back then, everybody got a job in the parking lot. I'd say about 20 pros would show up looking for caddies. Back then players would change caddies all the time and everybody would usually work. Nowadays with the money, the players tend to keep it in the family. A guy brings in a cousin, brother-in-law, a good friend from college. When you get to a tournament, you'll see guys with over 100 years of combined experience and they can't find work. It's sad. Bobby and I missed the cut that first weekend in Hartford. He paid me $300 and I thought it was great. We stayed together from there, but he didn't play a lot so I tried to pick up jobs in between. I worked for a bunch of different guys until I got really lucky and hooked up with Stuart Appleby in March of '97."

—JOEY DAMIANO

I grew up in Connecticut and I wanted to travel a little. I'd never gotten past New Jersey, so I decided to head out to California for a change of scenery. My cousin, Ken Green, was on the Tour, so I had made some plans to just hang out and watch him. My second week there he asked me if I wanted to caddie for him and I said, "Sure!" We were together on Tour for the next three years. Then, in 1990, I got together with Fred Couples and we've been together ever since."

—JOE LACAVA

I was working in a glass factory in Portland and wasn't happy with my job. Beginning in 1975, I caddied at my local club once a year when the LPGA came through to play. By the fall of 1980, I just boogied out of there without letting anyone know. I jumped on a bus with this guy I met and we went down to San Jose to caddie. I managed to get Betsy King's bag and she made the cut. I didn't get paid very well for that week, but what did I know? I was only 23 and I had no fear. By the Spring of '81 I was doing it full time."

—JERRY "SKYSCRAPER" SCHNEIDER

In 1985 I packed up my wife and our one-year-old son and headed out to a PGA Tour event. I hung out in the parking lot all week but I didn't manage to get a job. In an effort to make some money, I worked doubles in the pro-am. The temperature was around 100 degrees, the heat index was around 110, and the humidity was something like 80 percent. It was unbearable. I was carrying two bags for the first time in my life. Not knowing any better, I drank a Coca-Cola and then another Coca-Cola and then yet another. It never crossed my mind that I should try drinking water. By the time I walked off the 11th tee box with two bags on my back, my entire body went into cramps. It was the worst heatstroke ever. Once you've had it, you're more susceptible to it, and I've had it three or four times since then. Once that happened, I just went down. Of course, I couldn't continue. They took me to the clubhouse and iced me down and started making me drink water. When I got back to the hotel, I remember my wife rubbing me down for hours. I was laying on the bed and my calves were cramping up and there was nothing I could do about it. The pain was unbearable. **I remember thinking that maybe I'd made a mistake coming out here to land a bag.**

"On Thursday I came back to the golf course feeling much better. Turns out Mike Smith was having problems with his caddie, so when he fired him on Thursday I was in the right place at the right time and I got the bag. He played poorly on Thursday, three or four over. But he played fairly well on Friday.

He missed the cut, but just barely. Apparently I did well enough that he asked me to go to the BC Open the next week. I met a couple of other caddies traveling in a van and hopped in with them on Sunday afternoon and off we went to Endicott, New York, while my wife and child headed back home. Mike played great. The first day he shot a couple under, and on the second day he holed down an 8 iron from about 145 yards or so on the 18th hole for eagle. That put him in a tie for the lead. So I'm thinking, 'Man, this is the greatest thing ever to come along since sliced bread.' I was excited.

"I remember that Saturday round like it was yesterday. You have to get into a golf cart and ride down to the range to warm up. We drove down there—and of course, I had never been in a situation where my player was tied for the lead and in the last group of the day. I was nervous as hell. I couldn't have said shit if my mouth was full of it. I could tell that Mike was nervous as well. Then he hit some balls and it's the same way coming back. There wasn't a word. Of course, on the first hole he made a double bogey and didn't have a very good day—I think he shot 76. We tumbled off the leader board. We ended up finishing up the week OK. I learned from that experience that if you're nervous as a caddie, it definitely transfers over to your player. As a caddie, you don't have to hit the shot so you really shouldn't be nervous. **All you need is to have faith in your player. It's the greatest deal in the world.** I get to call the shots or help call the shots and be involved in the game, but ultimately it's not on me. It's on the player. I just have to do my best to keep my player from overthinking. If I would have known all that back then, I probably could have helped Mike win that tournament."

—KENNY BUTLER

    My first bag was with Mark Wiebe in the late '80s. To be honest, it wasn't that difficult to get a bag back then. You could just show up in the parking lot and you were pretty much guaranteed to find some work. I'd met Mark once before. He told me that if I ever wanted a job, to give him a call. I called him up just after Christmas and he told me to meet him in Hawaii in January. The first week in January, we played the Hawaiian Open and finished in the top 10, which got us into the next week. He didn't have his card but he played really well on the West Coast. In Los Angeles, he racked up another top-10 finish. We just kept on rolling from there. He made enough money that he could keep getting into different tournaments. He got into TPC and he got into Hilton Head. He was pretty successful.

"It was one of those things where you've never worked for the guy before, you just make an off-chance call, and it works out. It also helped that we got along so well. It wasn't that I was such an amazing caddie, it was just my turn for some luck to be thrown my way. It's like when you get fired—you just know the next guy that picks up the bag is going to the top 10 with him. I can't even count how many times that has happened. That probably explains why caddies get fired so often."

—Mark Chaney

    Like most veteran caddies, when I first started out, my only thought was that I'd like to do it for a tournament or two. Famous last words. I used to work in the athletic department at the University of Nevada. I knew a bunch of guys on the golf team and we used to joke around that I'd caddie for them if they ever made it to the Tour.

"I got burned out on my job, took a sabbatical and was living at my parents' place in Los Angeles. The L.A. Open was going on, so I headed over to the course to see what it was all about. All of the action was in the parking lot. Caddies left and right were asking players if they needed someone. Every once in a while, a player would say, 'Yeah, come on, let's go.' I thought, 'Heck, I can do that.' But there was nothing available. It was already Wednesday —late for an unknown caddie to find a player in the lot.

"The next weekend the Tour was playing in Monterey, California, so I crashed at a friend's place up there, bought a yardage book and hung out in the parking lot. 'I'll give it another go,' I thought. It was a Monday and my luck was better this time. The first guy I asked said, 'Yeah, sure, come on. Grab the bag. Let's go.' Great words for a wannabe caddie to hear. I didn't recognize the guy, but it turns out it was Tommy Aaron, the 1973 Masters champ. It went great. I enjoyed it. But it could have gone just a little better because he missed the cut.

"Next stop: San Diego. My parking lot approach was getting better and better and I quickly hooked up with David Thore. He was fresh out of Q-School and we managed to make the cut. I was hooked. I just kept on going from there, following the Tour wherever it went. Back then, you could do that. You can't do that now. When I didn't have a steady bag, I worked for CBS as a ball spotter. Chuck Wills, who worked for CBS, managed to keep a lot of hungry caddies fed by hiring them as spotters.

"One Wednesday I was just hanging out down by the bag room and Mike Reid showed up without a caddie. He came over, introduced himself, and asked me if I wanted to work for him that week. I didn't have to think twice about it. Nicknamed "Radar" for his outstanding driving accuracy, Reid was a solid player and a great bag to have back in the mid-1980s. I ended up working for him for 6½ years. By that time, caddying had become my career. **Getting a player like him at that time sealed the deal for me.**"

—Chuck Mohr

I received a full golf scholarship to the University of Mississippi and worked my way up through the ranks to play golf professionally. When I could no longer compete at a high level, I started caddying for a friend of mine from college, Gary Hallberg. Gary was the first four-time, first-team All-American in the history of intercollegiate golf. He was also the first player to earn his PGA card by winning a set level of money instead of going to Q-School. Working for him was a great way to start my caddying career."

—Anthony Wilds

My first official bag was with Craig Stadler at the 1973 U.S. Amateur Open at my home course, Inverness. It was amazing—Craig went out and won the damn thing. I had no intention of caddying full time. I did it off and on for the next six years. In fact, I quit Stadler twice to work on the Alaska pipeline because working up there was like finishing top five every week as a caddie (the purses were obviously a little smaller back in the '70s). In 1979, the U.S. Open was back at my home course at Inverness, so I figured it would be a great place to end my caddying career. We'd go out, win it (again), and I could move on to something else. We were doing all right on cut day and he made a shot that landed near the green on the 15th hole. For some reason we just couldn't find that ball. In all my years with Craig we'd never lost a ball. About 100 people poured out of the grandstand to help us find it, but we had no luck. The official ruled it a lost ball and he had to take a stroke. He ended up making a double bogey and that really took the wind out of his sails. He missed the cut and it really left a bad taste in my mouth. I couldn't have my last tournament be missing the cut in my hometown. So three-plus decades later I'm still doing it. **I owe it all to a ball that mysteriously disappeared over the edge of a green.**"

—"ALASKAN" DAVE PATTERSON

In the late '70s, I worked in a pro shop in Chicago and would head down to Phoenix in the wintertime to escape the cold. I loved golf and I started caddying at the Phoenix Country Club. When the Phoenix Open came around one year, I worked it as a caddie. I enjoyed it so much that I followed the Tour to the West Coast and back over to Florida. When the winter and spring tournaments were done and it came time to go back to my job in Chicago **I figured working six hours a day outside was better than working 12 hours in a pro shop.** I have been caddying ever since."

—DAVE "REPTILE" LEMON

I was at a point in my life where I'd lost two women in a really short period of time—my mother died and my wife and I went through a divorce. I desperately needed some sort of change in my life. I decided that caddying might be the answer. I knew Jerilyn Britz, the 1979 U.S. Open winner. She had been a teacher at my high school. I went to watch her play at a local tournament one weekend. After her round I talked to her and asked if I could be her caddie for the following weekend. She said yes, so I quit my job, left Minnesota, and didn't come back for 23 years."

—DICK "THE ANGEL" MARTIN

Technically, **the first time I ever caddied was when I was eight years old.** I guess you could say that from the time I was physically able to carry a bag I started caddying. But the first time I ever caddied on Tour was for my brother in the 1976 Texas Open in San Antonio. I was still a little green and probably wasn't quite as professional as I should have been. We started on the back nine on Thursday, and I remember we were paired with George Archer. We were standing on the fairway of the 15th hole (our sixth). The hole was a par-5 for the members, but they moved us up and we played it as a long par four. After a good drive, Bruce asked me about his second shot. He said, 'Is it a little 3 iron or a big 4 iron?' I said, 'Hell, I don't know. I'd be 25 yards back hitting a 3 wood!'"

—Brian Lietzke

In 1988 I decided I'd give it a try. I went down to Anheuser-Busch and stood out in the parking lot on a Monday morning 'meet and greet,' as the caddies liked to call it. It wasn't much fun standing out there with other caddies, watching the pros pull in. When I saw an opening I took it, introduced myself to Woody Blackburn as he was getting out of his car, and asked him if he had anybody for the week. Fifteen minutes later we were out on the course. Woody missed the cut by one stroke, but that was probably the best he'd done in years."

—Dale McElyea

I started caddying when I was eight years old. I love it. My dad was a caddie. He and his four brothers supported themselves during the Depression by caddying. They got a dime a round back then. It must be in my blood.

"I've done a little better than a dime a round. Once I got $200 from a guy at Pebble Beach for *not* caddying. I was signed up to caddie for an amateur tournament. The caddie-master said, 'Listen, I have this guy from San Francisco. His brother sprained his knee and isn't sure whether he's going to be able to make it [to caddie the] tournament or not, but he needs somebody to go out for the practice round. If somebody comes in and needs someone for the week, I'll save them for you, but why don't you go out for a practice round with this guy?' It was my first time around Pebble Beach and the guy was a really good player. He let me pull all of his clubs for him and read all his putts. He shot even par and told me that he really liked the way I worked and that if his brother couldn't go, I was on board. I told him I'd be back tomorrow. The next day he told me, 'My brother got the OK from his doctor to go today, but here's $200 for just showing up in case I needed you.' That's the job I always want: the $200-a-day gig not to work."

—JOHN "DOC" ROMAN

My first PGA Tour event was the Kemper Open in Maryland with Dicky Pride. It really wasn't that memorable, as we missed the cut. But for some reason (which I still don't know), Dicky liked the way I worked so he asked me to caddie for him one more time. My second PGA Tour event couldn't have been bigger—the 2003 U.S. Open. Dicky was playing great and I was having the time of my life. We were tied for fourth going into the final round and I was looking forward to a lot of face time on TV and a big paycheck at the end of the day. It didn't really turn out the way that I'd planned. Dicky went on to shoot eight over that Sunday and we went from tied for fourth to tied for 28th. Don't count those chickens before they hatch."

—CHRIS "CRISPY" JONES

Once you learn to land a job, you have to learn how to keep it. And if you can't keep it, you have to learn how to lose it...gracefully. Dan and I have had our little fallouts here and there but technically I've never been fired. But I have more than enough friends who have."

—Greg "Piddler" Martin

Former longtime caddie David Rawls was once on Franklin Langham's bag. (Keep in mind that Rawls was one of the biggest characters on Tour.) Langham was the type of player who treated his caddie more like an employee than a trusted partner. Throughout the entire tournament he talked down to Rawls. Eventually it became too much for Rawls to deal with, and on the 17th hole at Doral, Rawls simply dropped the bag and quit. 'Even my daddy doesn't talk to me that way,' Rawls told him as he walked away."

—Chuck Hart

I've worked for a ton of guys but I've only been fired once. On several occasions I didn't get asked back to caddie for my pro the following week, but that's way different from being fired. Throughout my career I managed to piece together jobs wherever I could get them. Before I started full time with Loren Roberts back in 2001, I managed to work 33 tournaments with 13 different players.

"The one time I was officially fired was by Ian Leggatt. He was a very good friend of mine from the days of the Australian Tour and the Canadian Tour. In 2001, Ian got his card via the Nationwide Tour, and because we were friends he asked me to caddie for him out on the PGA Tour. Ian really wasn't playing all that well and I sensed a change might do us both some good.

Early that year out at Pebble Beach he called me up on Saturday night after missing yet another early exit from a tournament and said to me, **'I'm going to do something different this week.' I knew straight away what that 'something different' was but I decided to be a bit of a smart ass. So I responded, 'Something different? Great! Are you planning on making a cut?** Are your drives going to hit the fairway?' He didn't think it was that funny, but it made it easier for him to tell me he was getting a new caddie. It worked out pretty well for me in the end because later that year I picked up Loren Roberts' bag and I haven't put it down since. It's been the longest and best player-caddie relationship that I've ever had."

—GRAEME COURTS

" I've been fired quite a few times and, to be honest, I understand the reasons why. One time in particular stands out. I had been working for Tommy Armour for four years and things were going pretty well. We were at a tournament in Las Vegas and had a 12:30 tee time the next day. I thought, **'No problem. I can drink and gamble all night and still make the tee time.'** Big mistake. Keep in mind that Vegas is like heaven for the caddies. Sports and gambling are in our blood, so a Tour stop in Las Vegas can be like the perfect storm. You can imagine what kind of night I had.

"When I woke up the next day in my hotel room, the clock read 1:01. I was 31 minutes late and there were 32 messages waiting for me—14 on my hotel phone and 18 on my cell. I made my way out to the course and met up with Tommy at the turn. 'Hi,' he said, and he kept walking. His brother Sandy was carrying the bag and I got fired right then and there. I really couldn't blame him—I deserved to be fired. I had violated the first rule of the Caddie Credo: 'Show Up!' He told me that if I quit drinking, I could get my job back. Well, I didn't exactly quit drinking, but I managed to slow it down a little. Tommy hired me back four months later and eventually, I did quit drinking—and I haven't showed up late for work since."

—Tom Anderson

I was working for Fuzzy Zoeller on the Champions Tour and things were going great. In 2002 he won the Senior PGA at Firestone and less than a month later he fired me—out of the blue, no warning at all. Actually, he didn't really fire me. His manager did. The manager called me up and said that Fuzzy was going to make a change and Fuzzy would call me in a couple hours to explain why. Five years later, I'm still waiting for that call."

—Eric Schwarz

I have been fired, but thankfully not often. I've been lucky enough to work for basically three guys in almost 18 years. There are a lot of other names in there, but I worked for Curtis Strange for five years, Jeff Sluman for almost seven, and Steve Flesch for two. In between them, there are a bunch of guys who I picked up the bag for—for a week here or a week there when my pro wasn't playing. I've been fortunate enough that I haven't been fired a lot, but we've all been fired at least once or twice. If you haven't been fired, then you haven't really caddied.

"My philosophy on it is that if you pick the bag up, it's just a matter of time before you are forced to put it down. Some of us pick it up and don't think about that, but if you pick the bag up, you have to put the bag down eventually. In general, two years is a pretty long relationship. Three or four or five is really good. Then there are a handful of guys that have been working for 20-plus years for the same guy. It's all part of the business. You can't take offense to it. Getting fired is part of the business. It's always just a matter of time. All you can do is your best and just hope you win, that you're productive, and that you and your player do well together. **You can't be afraid to be fired.** If you start to worry about whether you're going to get fired or not, then you're not going to make clear decisions—and you have to make clear decisions in our job. You can't base your decisions on not being fired. You have make decisions based on the situation and on your gut instinct. Some guys are more difficult than others. Some players—maybe they're a little bit more fiery or volatile or known for being hard on caddies—will influence a caddie's decision on how to attack the course. I feel that if I don't give my opinion, if I don't say what's on my mind or if I don't give someone information with conviction, then I'm not doing my job—and for that I ought to be fired."

—MARK CHANEY

They can fire you for bad breath if they want to. Players don't really need a reason to change caddies. One caddie got fired because he picked his fingernails and the player didn't like it. Fortunately, I've only been fired once in my career. Unfortunately, it was by the No. 1-ranked female player on tour at the time, Lorena Ochoa. In hindsight, I really should have made a better effort to make that relationship work, considering all the millions she has made on the LPGA Tour since then and how *Time* magazine recognized her as one of the most influential humans on the planet."

—TOM THORPE

When a caddie is fired it is either well-deserved or completely unjust. In the middle of one summer, we were playing down at Anheuser-Busch and it was a billion degrees out. As we were going out to play, we were all trying to dump the extra weight out of our bags—rain suits, umbrellas, and any extra balls that we didn't need. The caddie in my group decided to bring only three balls. Sure enough, on the second hole par-5 his player dumps two in the water. You've never seen a caddie sweat so much. He was burning up and it wasn't because of the weather. His player had no idea that he was down to his last ball. On the next hole the player hit his tee shot out into the trees and nobody could find it. We looked for it for as long as we possibly could, but that ball was way out into the woods and there wasn't much chance of finding it. The caddie seemed to be going deeper into the woods as if to hide from his player, or maybe he was considering making a run for it. Eventually, the player gave up and said, 'Okay, I'll take the drop and move on.' Well, it wasn't that easy. The player got disqualified and they had to walk in off the course. I didn't see that caddie around for a while."

—John "Chief" Griffin

I've been fired for so many different reasons that it's sometimes hard to keep track. I've been fired because I didn't *see eye-to-eye* with a player. I've been fired because we *didn't click.* But the absolute best one was from Chris Riley. We were standing at the Masters—a pretty tough place to get fired at—and **he told me, 'We're at the end of our journey. It's not just from me. This is a family decision.' Which in my experience really means that the wife doesn't like you.** He made $2 million in the last two years that I worked for him and then the following year, without me, he made $200,000."

—Chip "Alabama" Carpenter

"**All that matters is that I've been hired one more time than I've been fired.**"

—ROCKY HOBDAY

"Most of the time you know when you're going to get fired. It's like an old girlfriend. You just start doing things that you didn't do before—you stop opening the door for her, you show up late for dates, you forget her birthday."

—HILTON "J.J." JAMES

"I've been fired several times but I never hold a grudge. Things have a way of working out. I was working for David Peoples and he missed the cut. When he came out of the clubhouse, he told me that I should find another job for the next week because he wasn't going to play, he was going take a break. So I took David's advice and picked up Tom Scherrer's bag for the week. It was the first time I ever caddied for him and he won the tournament. Peoples showed up and played (with another caddie, obviously), but he clearly didn't do as well as Tom did."

—JIM "SPRINGBOARD" SPRINGER

"I was working for Payne Stewart's brother-in-law, Mike Ferguson. We were paired with Tom Gray and his caddie was Three Finger Jerry. We were on the 13th hole of the Green Island Country Club in Columbus, Georgia. Tom was having a particularly bad round and Three Finger was doing his best to stay positive and help his player find his game. Tom hit his shot and it went well over the green. Everybody clearly saw that it went over the green, but Three Finger yells out 'Nice shot!' Now,

I don't think Three Finger was being sarcastic—I really think he thought it was a decent shot—but it didn't matter to Tom. He was furious. He looked at us, then back over at Three Finger and snapped, 'Oh yeah, well f— you, too!' Then he told Three Finger to walk up to the green, drop the bag, and walk away. He fired him right there. I felt sorry for him, but he probably wasn't going to make much money from that bag anyhow."

—JERRY "SKYSCRAPER" SCHNEIDER

I was caddying at the L.A. Open back in '78 and it was the first bag I ever landed on the Men's Tour. Back then everybody on the course wore white clothes, which made things in the distance a little difficult to judge because the white blended into the background. We were out in the middle of the fairway after the tee shots and I let my player hit thinking that the group in front of us was off the green. Well, they weren't. The next thing you know, I'm yelling 'FORE!' and the ball damn near hit a player. That player came charging off the green at us, mad as hell. My player was so shaken by the whole thing that he proceeded to double-bogey the hole and showed his frustration by snapping his putter head off. I was forced to find a new bag the next week."

—JERRY "SPEEDWAY" AIKIN

You never really know anymore when you might get fired. Players don't have to give you a reason. In Greensboro my pro asked me whether he should hit his 6 or his 7 iron. I said he should hit just a smooth 6. He hit it pin high but about 40 yards right over the green. He blamed me for picking the wrong club. I blamed him for making such a horrible shot. **He fired me right on the spot—and we still had 12 holes to go."**

—DAVE "REPTILE" LEMON

"I've been fired for many reasons, but it mostly boils down to the fact that I'm ugly and my jokes suck. But there was one episode from when I was working the Ladies Tour. I was in San Diego and my pro had her girlfriend on the course with us. Before I knew it, they were kissing and rubbing up all over each other. Now, normally a little lesbian action doesn't bother me all that much, but it just didn't seem right on the golf course, so I yelled out to them 'Get a Room!' She yelled back, 'You're Fired!'"

—BILL "JUNKMAN" JENKINS

"I was working a pro-am with Roger Maltbie back when we were the best of friends. He kept giving me shit about my ability to caddie properly, [saying] that I was costing him shots. I told him that if I was so bad he should get another guy. He agreed. He fired me, hired himself, and carried the bag for the last two holes."

—JEFF "BOO" BURRELL

"Frank Lickliter called me up one day and asked me to work Houston for him. Just like that we go out there and we're in the top 10. I worked for him for the next couple of tournaments and things were going pretty well, but he'd already promised a couple tournaments down the road to a caddie named Australian Tony. I really thought that in the end I was going to be the permanent guy on the bag for Frank. Then, when it came time for him to make a decision on who was to be his caddie, he told me, 'This is a hard decision. I like you and Tony equally, but **my wife likes Tony's accent so I'm going to go with him.'**"

—BOB "MR. CLEAN" CHANEY

"I've been fired many times but the one I remember most happened when I was working for a Korean player on the Ladies Tour. We were playing in New Rochelle, New York, and I threw my back out just before we teed off on Thursday. There was absolutely no way that I could work that weekend; I could barely manage to get out of bed. I was a little worried that I would lose that bag for future tournaments, but she told me, 'Jeff, don't worry, I'm not going to fire you.' Three days later she called me up to tell me that I'm fired! The following week she won without me. That's OK, though—she hasn't done anything since."

—Jeff "the Shadow" Jones

"One week I was working for Robin Walton on the Ladies Tour and we were tied for the lead on Sunday. The wind had picked up a little and I knew that she wasn't much of a wind player. What I could never have known was that by the end we would have used up all our balls and shot an 86. She wanted me to go to Hawaii with her the next week (talk about windy!) and I said no thanks."

—Bill "Junkman" Jenkins

"Greg Twiggs is a great guy. I love him to death. He's a big ol' guy, maybe 240 pounds. During one tournament he just kept pissing and moaning the whole time. Finally, I'd had enough and I told him to 'Just play golf, God Almighty!' He had been complaining about the fairways being too narrow and the wind catching his ball. I told him it would be helpful if he'd quit whining and hit the damn ball straight—then there wouldn't be any need for complaining. I got so sick of it, that I took two cigarettes, broke them off and put the filters in my ears. He didn't notice for a while, but then he asked me, 'What do we got to the front?' I said, "What?" He said, 'What do we got to the front?' I said, 'Huh?' 'What the f— do we have to the front?' Then he saw what I was doing. I took the filters out and said a final, 'What?' He said, 'You know, this is our last f—ing day together.'"

—"REEFER" RAY REAVIS

Sometimes getting fired is the furthest thing from your mind because things seem to be going great. On the other hand, getting fired can be predictable—like the few times I've been fired for missing tee-times. The ones that really hurt are the ones you don't expect. A few years ago I was fired by a guy right out of left field. He earned his card for the first time in four years and made over a million dollars. Three weeks into the season after making the last two cuts in a row he walked out of the locker room with a check in one hand and the other outstretched to shake my hand. He told me that he needed a fresh face and that all good things must come to an end. To this day I still have no idea why."

—"ALASKAN" DAVE PATTERSON

I've been fired more times than I care to count. But for me it's never been a big surprise. I've always been able to predict the end. There are some very clear signs that you need to watch out for. The conversation will shift a little, the jokes won't be as funny, and the player will stop answering your questions and engaging in conversation. When the end is near, your player will toss the clubs at your feet instead of handing them back to you. Soon you start to feel like you're living under a microscope, and that even the smallest of tasks seem difficult. You start feeling clumsy and have trouble finding things in his bag that he needs. All the while he's just staring at you and you get the impression that he just can't wait to fire you. **When the end finally comes, it's as much a relief to you as it is to the player.**

—LINN "THE GROWLER" STRICKLER

Three

NOT LIKE THE OLD DAYS

All of the old-time caddies say the same thing: back in the day, it was easy to find a job. You'd just hang out in the parking lot and sooner or later you'd find a player for the week. Or when your regular player took the week off you could pick up another bag to earn some extra money. That doesn't happen anymore. Now the money is so high that full-time caddies don't have to get off-week jobs to survive and they treasure their downtime at home. Back in the good old days, guys who became caddies were usually running from something so they'd just keep moving around the country from tournament to tournament. The road became our home. We sure as hell weren't in it for the money.

When I started out, I got $200 a week. First prize in a tournament was $50,000. So if your player won the tournament, you'd get $200 and your 10 percent cut which would be $5,000. Only one guy out of a field of 156 would make that kind of money; everybody else would be making much, much less. If you were right on the cut line on Friday, you'd hope not to make it because if you just barely made the cut it was highly unlikely you'd get a top-10 finish so you'd be working two more days for basically nothing. Last place on the weekend only brought in $800 so your cut of that would not pay for your food and lodging for those extra two nights, not to mention the drinks at the bar. These days last place can bring in $50,000, so you sure as hell want to do everything you can to make the cut.

We'd try to save the money we made during the summer months to get by in the off-season. A bunch of us used to head down to Indian Rocks Beach, Florida, to ride out the winter. We'd get a hotel and stay three guys to a room. If you had a couple grand saved, you could make it until the season started up again. After two months off, we couldn't wait for things to get going again. On the West Coast, the tournaments start in Hawaii and end in Los Angeles, then the East Coast swing starts in Miami. As soon as Sunday night came in Los Angeles, four of us would jump in a car and bust our asses on Interstate 10. Stops were only allowed to pee, eat, and get gas. We'd get no sleep or shower and pull into Miami on Tuesday morning ready to go. Now we're a little more spoiled. We can actually fly from event to event.

The money has changed the Tour in some other major ways. There's been a huge influx of the Johnny-come-lately caddies who are friends or relatives of the player. They're the "MCI" caddies (on the friends and family plan). Players don't have as much fun as they used to. They walk around like robots now. They have the latest equipment, the most advanced technological gadgets; they're burdened down with all these little gimmicks to make them "better." One equipment guy tried to sell me a tool for finding elevation. I told him that I'd been playing that hole for 25 years. I know that Dan [Forsman] hits a six iron 170 yards and I know that the last seven years we've played this hole, he's hit a six iron 20 times and it's gone 162 yards, so obviously this hole plays eight yards longer. Now they have machines to tell you all of that information so the caddies are turning into robots, too. Another major change has been the invention of the mass-produced yardage book. For $20 you can buy a book that tells you everything a caddie needs to know: how far it is to every bunker, every sprinkler, the front of every green, and all of the elevations. But even with that book, I'll still walk the course to make sure it's right. Old habits are hard to break. In the old days, we made the book ourselves. It was a lot more work, but a lot more fun.

The biggest change is that caddies used to be like a family. We not only hung out together all the time but we looked out for each other. Now guys are so fiercely competitive they'll do anything they can to get a leg up on the competition, especially when it comes to protecting their jobs.

Finally, the PGA Tour has morphed into a world tour. Forty percent of the guys on Tour are from other countries and naturally they bring their caddies with them. The Australians are with the Australians, the South Africans run with the South Africans, and the Europeans stick with the Europeans—the Tour is much more divided than it used to be. And the caddies of my generation are fading away.

"Today's caddies think that they should be given gifts. Back when we first started we were barely getting by. We had nothing. In fact, **it was so bad that at Tour events they had signs that would say 'Public Welcome, Caddies Not Allowed.'** The younger caddies that come out now take everything for granted. They think they're supposed to get all the breaks in the world. They have no idea how good they have it."

— JEFF "BOO" BURRELL

"   When I won my first tournament with Gene Sauers he won $81,000. That's not even a top 10–finish purse these days."
    —JIM "SPRINGER" SPRINGBOARD

"   Back then we were so broke that we would go eight to a room. I even knew a guy that would sleep in construction sites. Things could get tense in those motel rooms. I remember one time around 4:00 AM a guy went to the bathroom—the only problem was that he was still standing in the main room when he did it, and pissed on the six guys sleeping on the floor. Did I mention there was a little bit of drinking going on back then as well?"
    —BILL "JUNKMAN" JENKINS

"   Back when we started in the late '70s, if you managed to finish your first year you were quite something—because **it sure wasn't the money that kept us going.** My first year we finished fourth in a tournament and I made a whopping $225."
    —JERRY "SPEEDWAY" AIKIN

"   The game is more scientific now, but the bottom line is that golf was never meant to be a science and never will be. You can hit two perfect 7 irons and they won't go the same distance. It's a feel game, and the older experienced caddies understand this."
    —DALE MCELYEA

"   **Now caddies have rental cars, fly on corporate jets with their players, and stay at the Ritz-Carlton.** It used to be that after our round we'd all meet up at the local dive bar and

Loren Roberts talking with Graeme Courts at Boeing on the Champions Tour

dissect the day's events. Now the young caddies hurry back to their hotel rooms with their expensive new laptops to check on scores and stocks. But a bunch of us older guys still manage go to the same bars and same motels we were going to 20 years ago."

—HILTON "J.J." JAMES

When Tiger came out in '96, things changed dramatically. Now the money is much higher, so the players are totally different. You can't go out and have a beer and some fun with them anymore. They're too busy exercising and bringing their friends and relatives out to caddie for them.

"You never really know when you might get fired. Players don't have to give a reason to fire you anymore. The days of

59

sharing motel rooms, driving back and forth all over the country, and speeding down the highways all night just to barely make it in time for the next tournament are over. Today the Nationwide Tour is the way the PGA used to be."

—DAVE "REPTILE" LEMON

It is so night-and-day how the caddies are treated now compared to how we were treated in the early '80s. These young guys have to be kidding me when they bitch and complain about stuff. They have no idea how good they have it."

—TOM JANIS

The year was 1981 and I was at an event at Marsh Creek Plantation in South Carolina. They kept the caddies in a roped-off pen. If you dared to leave the pen they escorted you off the grounds. We did have a Port-O-John in the fenced-off area which was a classy touch. As if being kept in a cage all day wasn't bad enough, we had to wear white jumpsuits at all times. It was so damn hot outside and we were absolutely swarmed by hordes of damn sand flies. At least now we have the Caddie Trailer, which is air-conditioned and full of good food, and a whole safe zone we can hang out in and be by ourselves. I sure don't miss those stupid jumpsuits and swarming flies."

—JERRY "SKYSCRAPER" SCHNEIDER

A big part of caddying used to be getting the numbers. Walking off the yardages isn't as easy as it sounds. You had to possess the skill of walking around a pond in the middle of a hole and figuring out what the right yardage was to get across it. All of that is gone now. Being able to accurately walk yardage was a skill that a caddie had to have. It's an art that is totally lost. Now we have a yardage book that is perfect every week and lasers to shoot everything. Then your player would have to trust your numbers because you literally paced it. When we went to St. Andrews, there were no sprinklers. You'd stand in the middle of the fairway and tell your player to aim for the third steeple on the left. That was your yardage point. Now that's real golf."

—"MINNESOTA" MIKE LEALOS

We used to have a lot more camaraderie with our peers. If a guy was in trouble we'd always help him out. **We were always getting together, playing softball games, going to parties, and having community keg parties. There was a lot of drinking going on back then, that's for sure.** Now there's a sense of insecurity in the air and it seems like people will go to any length to stab you in the back in order to get a bag."

—JERRY "SKYSCRAPER" SCHNEIDER

When I first started, it was mostly black caddies. The pay was terrible and the benefits were nothing. Now, with the bigger money, the players are bringing their friends and relatives out to caddie for them. It isn't easy for the professional caddies with years of experience anymore."

—RICHARD "JELLY" HANSBERRY

When I started out 24 years ago there were a lot of guys escaping society. Today's caddies are college educated and have special skills. You'll find more college degrees carrying the bags than hitting the balls."

—ANTHONY WILDS

The equipment changes have been devastating. It's primarily the golf balls now, but the clubs also play a role. People say that nobody used to hit like they do today. That's just not true. There were guys that did hit it like that. The difference was that they couldn't hit it straight so they would never find their golf balls. There were guys that were averaging 290–300 in our day. But they were wild, because the equipment just didn't work at that speed. The wooden drivers had bulge and roll on them.

"The kids these days, well, they're all great players, I'm not knocking them. But the equipment has dramatically changed the game. You used to have to spin the ball both ways to play good golf. Now they just hit it high and straight. They just kill it. Not that they can't hook it if they hit it behind a tree or something. They still know how to hit hooks. When we played, it was smaller greens and firmer conditions. To get to a left pin, you had to land in the middle of the green and spin it left. You couldn't just take the ball straight up in the air and land it in there. It didn't work. It's much more of a power game now. The equipment manufacturers are so involved and they've got so much research and development invested that I think it would be really tough to get them to cooperate, like how Major League Baseball doesn't allow metal bats. In my opinion, the technology doesn't do the average guy a lot of good, unless you've got a swing speed that's in the 120 miles per hour range. But for some of these pros, the new technology can make a world of difference. Bubba Watson averaged 355 off the tee at Colonial. That's just nuts."

—CHUCK HART

"These days everybody thinks they're a f—ing all-star. I've been poor all my life and money ain't gonna change me. When I first started on the Tour, we all watched out for each other. Now guys are always bitching about something like, 'Argh, they're not feeding us this week'. Wah, wah, wah. These are the same guys who never had to stand in a parking lot looking for a job or beg to get a gig as a TV spotter for 35 bucks a day. All that complaining gets old pretty damn fast."

—"REEFER" RAY REAVIS

"Back when I started out in the '70s, only the top 60 were exempt, rather than the current top 125. This made things a lot more interesting in the Monday qualifiers. There were lots of so-called 'rabbits' following the tour and qualifying for the tournaments on Mondays, which made the job of landing a bag in the parking lot easier. Players showed up without a caddie all the time. Not anymore. Everybody knows well in advance who will play in the tournament and who their caddie will be. Now we just have a four-spot Monday qualifier so they can still officially call it an 'open', but it isn't truly an 'open' like it used to be."

—"ALASKAN" DAVE PATTERSON

"Because the money is so much higher, guys are playing in fewer tournaments. It used to be they played every week and had to qualify on Mondays. So the schedule was a lot tougher than what it is now. The first tournament Bruce won was in 1977 and the prize was $40,000. **Last year 70 players made over a million dollars.** The caddies usually take 10 percent and as much as 15 percent for top-10 finishes. Not bad for carrying around a golf bag."

—BRIAN LIETZKE

Here's my girl Donna Earley, with her pro, Jennifer Rosales at the Women's World Cup in South Africa.

"Over 30 years ago, Angelo Argea, who was caddying for Jack Nicklaus, began to blaze the trail for today's modern caddies. He was really the first technical kind of a caddie. Angelo was getting yardages and walking the courses early in the mornings before anyone else had ever thought of caddying as a career. Even when it went beyond walking the courses, when it got sophisticated enough to prepare an accurate yardage book, Angelo already knew everything that Jack needed to know. Now everybody's got the yardage book and the lasers for exact distances. Nearly all the caddies now are former players—not just average players but great players who just didn't have what it takes to make it on Tour. The guys that caddied in the old days weren't really golfers. They'd just gotten out of the service or were looking for some action. Angelo was a taxi driver in Las Vegas who kind of conned his way into the job. Most caddies today have all got to be good players so that they can better relate with and truly be partners with their players."

—CHUCK HART

When I first started out on the Tour 30 years ago we would caddie, then go party, then caddie, and then party again. I could drink until two or three in the morning and be up for my tee time, no sweat. Now I can't rebound from a night of partying; I need my eight hours of sleep in order to be sharp in the morning. I guess that means I'm getting old."

—ERIC SCHWARZ

We'd go four guys to a room at the Motel 6 and the high scores got the rug. At least now you get your own bed."
—"MINNESOTA" MIKE LEALOS

When guys like me first started out as caddies in the '70s, this was not so much of a job as it was a lifestyle. It was a way to travel, it was a way to party, it was a way to see the world. The guys that come on Tour now—whether it is through a college buddy or brother-in-law or whatever—they're guys that may have college degrees and decent jobs where they might make around $50,000 a year. Out here, a caddie can make that in one week. The money has changed things. Because of that, you don't have the characters you used to have. They've been weeded out. If you're going to pay someone six figures to caddie for you, you don't need someone who's hungover in the morning with uproarious tales from the night before. You expect more out of your caddie than just being a transient hobo who's traveled around America.

"I'd say because of the money—so basically, because of Tiger—caddies are changing. We've had to change. We can't be the same people we used to be because the players pay us enough money that they expect more than a vagabond on the bag, not that there's anything wrong with drunken vagabonds. In the late '80s my boss always wanted to know what I'd done the night before. He was married with kids and he got a kick out of my stories. Did I meet a girl? Did I get in a fight? What time did I get home? Now if a caddie shows up hungover, the pro will just look at you like, 'What the hell do you think you're doing? Six figures a year for you to get two hours of sleep and come to work in bad shape?' This new crop of caddies is so one-dimensional. They caddie, they go work out, and then they go back to the room, get on their computers, and start playing online poker. Our days used to consist of caddying, heading back to the motel, showering (maybe), and then meeting up and drinking at the closest bar until they kicked us out."

—AL MELAN

"Twenty-five years ago they didn't have enough caddies to do the job. Nobody wanted those jobs because the pay was low and everything was hard. I remember caddying at the Riviera in L.A. back in '83. We had a good tournament and finished fifth. There was no caddie transportation shuttle back to your car or your hotel after a certain time, so if you played late you just missed the last shuttle and that was that. So I had to try to hitch a ride back with the public and it took me over 4½ hours to go the four or five miles back to my car because of the traffic jams leaving the course. **Now we can valet park**

at Wachovia and at Greensboro, and if you make the cut on the weekend, you can park in the player's parking lot. Talk about progress!"

—ANTHONY WILDS

"You've got to work hard to keep your job and protect and take care of it for all you're worth. There are at least five caddies in the parking lot each week that have 10 years each of experience and plenty of wins under their belts. Nobody is handing out jobs anymore. And these days, players are friends with their caddies much more than they used to be. There was a time when we'd never go out to eat with our player. We didn't want to be under his thumb; we'd already been out there working for him for eight hours. Now you see players and caddies together out for dinner and hanging out in the local casinos. Probably because they are all related now. Which I guess would explain the lack of jobs in the lots too."

—BOB "MR. CLEAN" CHANEY

"Cell phones have changed our job drastically. When I used to work for Tommy Armour—this was pre-cell phone days—we'd call our player at the hotel the night before and find out what time we were supposed to meet them. It was very often that he'd say, 'I'll see you at 9:00 AM,' and then roll in at 1:00 in the afternoon. So I'd sit around and wait for four hours. Without fail, as soon as I'd go out to walk around the golf course and check some holes, he'd finally show up and start asking the other caddies where the heck I was. So **when cell phones came along my life got a lot easier. A lot of the waiting around has been taken out of our job."**

—TOM ANDERSON

Television coverage has changed everything, especially the Golf Channel. I didn't think that dedicating an entire channel to our sport was possible but it clearly has worked and it has been the best thing for our sport. The mobile camera came along and it changed the golf landscape for the viewer at home. They used to just have cameras positioned to the left or the right of the greens and behind the tee boxes, but now the experience for the viewer is second to none. It's like they are right there in the game."

—LINN "THE GROWLER" STRICKLER

Obviously the biggest change is the money. That's huge. When I started some 25 years ago, most tournaments had three or four $100,000 purses. There were maybe a couple of big $500,000 tournaments. Back in 1985, when Joey Sindelar won the B.C. Open, I was working for Mike Reid who finished second by himself. My roommate was working for Billy Glasson and he finished third. I think Joey got $54,000 for first place, Mike got $39,000 for second, and Billy Glasson got around $27,000 for third. My roommate and I thought we had died and gone to heaven. That was a huge payday for us. Back then, the tournaments were put on by cities and organizations; it wasn't corporate golf so there wasn't all that sponsorship money. Now as caddies we make about what the players made back then. These days $300,000 is third place, maybe fourth place in some tournaments. I've heard people complain that the money has gone up too high. But I don't think the purses are too much now.

"Take a look at the world of sports. **This is the only one that is a pure sport in our country.** If a player comes to a tournament and misses the cut, then he doesn't make anything.

He makes zero money. In fact, he *loses* money: he still has to pay his caddie his weekly salary. He still has to pay for his hotel. He still has to pay his airfare and all his expenses. There's no appearance money. So golf, in that respect, is a pure sport. You make your money based on how good you are every single week. You can't sign a five-year deal with a team as a bench sitter and make $1 million a year and not contribute. So I think whatever the guys earn, they deserve. It's purely based on performance. You have basketball players and baseball players making $15 million a year and playing with a guaranteed salary. Golf is small compared to all that. Obviously, you've got Tiger and maybe the top five guys, but even Tiger's big year has been what, $10 million? Obviously, he's a unique player, so you have to put him in a category with Jordan, where he's making $100 million a year just in endorsements. But he has certainly earned all that.

—CHUCK MOHR

Technology has changed the game. When I first started out we didn't have the 60-degree wedge. I remember the trouble players first had using it. They would hit it fat, they would leave it short, and they just hated it. They'd swear to never use that club again. Now they've figured out just how versatile that club is, how it can get them out of tighter spots. The same can be said for the new drivers and new golf balls. Technology has without a doubt made the game easier."

—JOHN "CADILLAC" CARPENTER

After rounds we used to go to the bar; now caddies go to the gym."

—ARTIE GRANFIELD

"When I look at today's players I don't even think they need caddies. The players are so good and so knowledgeable about the courses, compared to 20 years ago when guys would just show up and play. Now the yardage is exact, they use lasers for measurements. They can probably even study the layout of the course online before they show up to play it. I think the caddying has been taken out of the game. Now all you have to do is shut up and count the money."

—JOHN "CHIEF" GRIFFIN

"I guess it's still possible to get a job by hanging out in the parking lot for eight hours on a Tuesday because alternates might get into the tournament if others pull out due to injuries. **It seems today that even the first 15 alternates have their own caddies.**"

—DAVE "REPTILE" LEMON

"**When I first started, not only did we have so many guys to a motel room that we'd go low score for the day to see who gets the bed, but the last guy out of the shower in the morning had to use the bed sheet to dry off.**"

—ERIC SCHWARZ

"Guys used to have great nicknames. Now they are all so serious, or worse, they are closely related to the player. **Somehow the great tradition of the nickname is starting to fade away.**"

—GREG " PIDDLER" MARTIN

FOUR

NICKNAMES ON TOUR

CADDIE CREDO #4:
"Nicknames are given, not chosen."

It's important to know that in the caddie world, nicknames are given, not chosen. Nobody was better at handing out nicknames than the legendary Bruce Edwards, Tom Watson's longtime caddie. Bruce had an amazing ability to watch a new guy for a while and then hit him with the best nickname that was sure to stick with the guy for the rest of his life. Sometimes the names were as simple as where the guy was from, in order to not get confused by guys with the same name i.e., Irish Dave and Scottish Dave. (Come to think of it, sometimes we'd get them confused anyway because their accents were similar.) The best ones have the ability to sum a guy up with one word. It's a form of art.

I got my nickname in Boston. A bunch of us were on our way to a Red Sox game and everyone had piled into the car. I was still in the motel room, getting ready to go, when Bruce yelled out the window, "Greg, stop piddling and get out here!" Thus, the "Piddler" was born.

People like to say it takes me an hour and a half to watch *60 Minutes*. Like I said, a good nickname will stick with you forever.

One of the most perfect nicknames out there is that of "Reefer" Ray Reavis. I could tell you how he got that name but he does a much better job of it. Read on.

A fellow by the name of Chuck Wills, God bless his heart, used to take care of us caddies by giving us jobs as spotters for television when we either didn't have a job that weekend or when we missed the cut. He'd pay us $35 a day and it kept us alive. Anyhow, I was working for Chuck after getting a total hip replacement. He put me on the 13th hole at Doral. I told him 'Chuck, this is f—ed man, you know I've got a broken hip and you're putting me the farthest away on the golf course.' Chuck replied, 'Ray, I want you out there, take my golf cart.' I was in no position to argue—something about not asking for toast when you're in the bread line—so off I went driving the back way to the 13th hole.

"I stopped to burn me one before I got to the hole. So I light up and I'm sitting there puffing away, I've got the headset on while I'm taking a couple of hits, when all of a sudden through the headset I hear Chuck yell, 'Put that shit out!' I take another little hit and I hear, 'I said put that out!' I'm looking around and still don't see anybody. I push a button and ask, 'Chuck where the hell are you?' He says 'The f—ing camera guy has you on TV in my golf cart and you're smoking that shit. Now bring that cart in!' So I put it out and I called in and said 'Chuck, I can't bring it in. I'm too high—I might hit somebody.' I still worked the full day and earned my $35. After all, I am a professional."

—"REEFER" RAY REAVIS

A Brief Glossary of Caddie Nicknames

Alaskan Dave is from Alaska, but we also call him **Hawaiian Dave** because he said he lived there too. When a lot of the guys first came out, we didn't get all that creative. We just went by where they were from. Thus we have Boston Mike, Alabama, the Brit, Montana, Rhode Island Tom…the list goes on and on.

Antman got his name because he's like an ant on the green. When he reaches down to read his putts, he gets down on all fours and lies down like an ant. We all complain and say that it's illegal, but apparently it's not.

B. He was always saying, "Be there or be square," so we started calling him "B".

Bamb is really shy and he just looks like a baby deer. We always joked that the really tough pros were going to make him cry.

Every single meal **Barbecue Bob** ate on Tour came off the grill.

Beautiful Bill was on the Ladies' Tour. He had a birthmark on his right ear, so he grew his hair long to cover it. Always, before the golfers would putt, he'd flip his hair back like a model.

Before working for Jan Stephenson, **Bruce the Star** was a practicing attorney in Washington, DC. One day he just said, "Screw this attorney stuff." Maybe he'd been in trouble, or maybe the Tour was just calling his name. Who knows.

Jan Stephenson was the first really sexy person in women's sports. She posed for *Playboy* and had posters made. None of the lesbians on tour liked her because she was different, but the LPGA loved it. Bruce ended up not only caddying for her, but being her agent. At tournaments he handed out not the nude photos but calendars and posters. He'd sell them for $20 and take $10 for himself. So we called him Bruce the Star. A lot of times when he'd come out with her, he'd bring the bag out and stand right by the ropes to be near all the fans. Most caddies stay far away from the ropes, but not Bruce the Star. He loved the attention.

Boats had shoes the size of Noah's Ark.

Bones is tall and lanky.

Boz looked exactly like Brian Bosworth, a popular football player at the time. He'd actually sign autographs for kids at the tournaments or the airport who thought he was "the Boz."

Whenever we ate out as a group, the moment it was time to pick up the check or leave the tip **Bullet** was out of there, faster than a speeding bullet.

Brother James looked just like Jesus. He had long hair past his shoulders, a full beard, and called himself Brother James. He really thought he was the son of God. He really did. He was just way out there, a wonderful man.

How did **Budweiser Paul** get his name? He drank Bud every night.

The first guy he ever caddied for was Dave Rummels, and they had such a memorably bad weekend that we started calling him **Bumbles**.

Baghdad Bob gets bombed every night.

Businessman Bill *claims* to be a businessman, but he's not a very good one. He dumped one player to go with Ben Curtis, and then shortly after, he quit Ben. The next week he found himself unemployed while Ben was busy winning the British Open.

At the Ryder Cup, Freddie Burns reads a putt with Hal Sutton and Scott Verplank.

It doesn't matter what city we're in. John **"Cadillac"** Carpenter is always driving a Cadillac.

He was constantly telling the rest of us that he was like a machine out on the course, never getting any yardages wrong. When we'd go out to a golf course that we'd never been to before, we'd go to the first tee, map it out, and do the yardage. Not the **Caddie Machine**. He would always do it backwards. He'd start on the 18th green and work backwards, because he said that's the way a golf ball would see it.

Chief is of Native American descent. We might have gotten his name from *One Flew Over the Cuckoo's Nest*, but I can't be sure of that.

Coach Walker coached guys all the time, whether they wanted it or not.

Complaino's real name is Andy Laino but all he does is complain. His guy would miss a four-foot putt and he'd come in and say, "Yeah, we should have easily won today."

Every time **Dancing Duk** would walk into the caddie area he would do a little two-step. I think he was just happy to see us.

Whenever we went out for drinks, **Deep Pockets** never could quite reach his wallet.

He came over from the Ladies Tour and I heard from a friend that they'd called him **Dufus** there. So when he showed up one week I said to him, "Hi, Dufus, nice to meet you." He got mad at me and said, "Don't you ever call me Dufus again!" A bunch of the other caddies overheard this, and it was Dufus from there on out.

Dirty Dan was a sneaky bastard. He used to have one of those scanners, the kind that picked up people's conversations. He always had gimmicks, like a watch that could turn a TV on and off. He'd go by guys' hotel rooms and change the channel from outside. He'd go into bars and if some guy was watching a soccer game, he'd turn it to the Packers game. His most famous antic was when he was working for Loren Roberts on the Ryder Cup team and was betting on the matches. That's Dirty Dan.

Detroit Slim, a fat guy from the Motor City.

It didn't matter if it was 90 degrees—**Downwind Vic** would always caddie with his trenchcoat on. He looked like Sherlock Holmes. And not only did he caddie in that thing, he *lived* in it. Some people say he was hit in the head by a golf ball and got goofy. Hence, Downwind Vic—you can smell him coming.

Disco is the best-looking guy on tour—and he knows it. He goes to all the discos, he twirls, and he dances. He's wears gold chains and earrings. He gets more girls than anybody else—he's the best I've ever seen.

Eag-Al: His name is Al and he's as bald as an eagle.

Froggy hopped around from caddie to caddie asking for a loan. "Can I borrow five?" "Do you got an extra ten?" You'd give him five bucks and then he'd hop right out of the room.

Golf Ball is a name of respect. He worked for Calvin Peete and he was truly an original.

The General liked to get drunk and boss us around, ordering us where to put our stuff, and saying things like, "My name's the General and all the rest of you are privates."

77

We started calling Brian Lietzke **"G.P."** because he would only show up to caddie guaranteed purse events.

Mr. Greenjeans used to come out to the course with these big green farmer's overalls and caddie in them all day. He reminded us of the guy on *Captain Kangaroo*.

He was the original **Gypsy**, but keep in mind, we were all gypsies back then. We were vagabonds, we didn't have homes, we lived out of motels, scrounging money to manage a ride to the next tournament.

In the late 1950s, **Jelly** was playing in a big championship baseball game at old Griffith Stadium in Washington, DC. He hit a ground ball somewhere between third and shortstop and ran as hard as he could to get to first. Somebody in the stands hollered out that he runs like a big, fat, jelly baby. His teammates picked up on it and the name has stuck ever since.

If anyone ever left something on his plate he could guarantee that **Junkman** would eat it. Coincidentally, he's in the trash business now.

Killer is a former boxer who had a surprisingly great record.

Last Call never left the bar before…you guessed it.

Mr. Clean looks just like the household cleaner guy.

Motorcycle Jim is unbelievable. Everywhere he goes, he drives a motorcycle. We'd go from L.A. to Miami and this clown's on a motorcycle. He also thought he could park in the fancy player parking lot because he had a motorcycle.

If there were a picture in the dictionary next to the word "nerd" you would find the **Nerd**.

Dale McElyea, president of the Professional Tour Caddies Association, doing his thing while Steve Lowery practices his putts. (Photo courtesy of McElyea)

No Pockets was the only guy worse than Deep Pockets.

No Truth: he never told the truth. Ever.

We called him **O.B.**, after Obi-Wan Kenobi. He was nice about it, but he had a tough time getting a job. No pro wants a caddie named O.B., out of bounds.

Pete the Pro was an older guy who came out from England. He told everybody that he used to be a golf pro and that he was just out here to help guys out and give them tips.

"Golf is more than just a game. It is mind over matter. It's about conquering self-consciousness. It's not just 'Gentlemen only, ladies forbidden.' It's more than that." Quite the philosopher, **Plato** is.

Preacherman carried that Bible with him everywhere he went and spread the gospel any chance he had.

Psychological Bob is a master analyst who used to work in a state hospital. Once he and another caddie were stuck at the top of a Ferris wheel in Williamsburg, Virginia. It was broken for over an hour. The whole time he sat there saying, "There's a reason for this. There's a time and a place for everything." He says that about everything.

We all call him **the Russian**, but his real name is Brad Kraznof. A Yale-educated attorney, he was one of the smartest caddies in history. In his spare time, he would study Russian.

Back in 1978, a bunch of caddies were playing down in Hilton Head. Dave was hitting the ball in all the ponds and hazards on hole after hole. One of the guys said he was like a reptile because he was playing in the water with the snakes and alligators more than he was playing on the course. He's been **Reptile** ever since.

The only time he'd ever talk was at night after about eight beers. His wife claims she married three people: Rick in the Morning, Transitional Rick, and **Rick at Nite**.

A lot of people guess the nickname has to do with drugs, but that's not it at all. We call him **Speedy** because he's from Indianapolis.

Squeaky has a really high-pitched voice.

We'd ask him how long he was going to stay out on tour and he'd say, "Oh, I'm just going to be out here for a short stint." After a few years, we just started calling him **Stint**. It was around that time that we started calling every new caddie "Stint" because they all had the same story. This wasn't their career, it was just something they were going to do for a very short period of time. Famous last words.

Stove Pipe smokes like a chimney.

Tel Aviv Sid? He's of Jewish descent.

Turnpike never spent money on a hotel. Whenever asked where he slept the night before, he'd say "on the turnpike." The road was truly his home.

When he first started out he had no luck getting a bag, so he worked as a spotter for the TV broadcasts—and the nickname **TV Tommy** was born.

Once he was looking for a ball in the rough and he accidentally kicked it. When you kick a ball, it's a two shot penalty. He cost his player and we never let **Two Shot** forget it.

Weed just loved to smoke.

The Wanderer had a motor home and he'd give us rides to the next tournament for $20. It was great because we could sit inside and drink beer and use the bathroom. He even had a barber's chair in there and he'd give us haircuts. But every time we'd stop to get gas we'd end up waiting 30 minutes because the son of a bitch wandered off somewhere.

White Shoes *always* wore white shoes.

FIVE

INSIDE THE ROPES

CADDIE CREDO #5:
*"Never let a black cat cross your path—
especially if the black cat is 'That Guy'."*

"That Guy" is a legend. He is the biggest "black cat" in the history of the Tour. Everybody said he was a jinx, but I never believed it until it affected me. In 1992, Dan [Forsman] was trying to make the Ryder Cup team and things were looking good. We had a three-shot lead and we were in the last group. Piece of cake. Just before our tee time, I saw "That Guy" standing with a bunch of the caddies. I went right up to him and rubbed his head in front of everybody in an attempt to disprove the legend. I really liked the guy and I was starting to feel bad for him. Guys were really starting to avoid him. "Wish me luck!" I said, as I released him from a headlock.

If we had shot even par, we would have won by five shots. Dan fired an embarrassing 82. There's no way around it—we were jinxed for the day and it was all my fault for tempting fate.

Another time we were at a tournament in Denver and there was a long rain delay with one hole left. Tony Navarro was caddying for Jeff Sluman and they were paired with us. Tony and I took off for an hour until the delay was over. As we headed back out to the course in a cart, we saw "That Guy" and he needed a ride. Tony said, "No! Do not pick him up. Don't do it." "Come on," I said, "he needs a ride." Besides, all Sluman had to do to make the cut was bogey the last hole. We picked up "That Guy'" and went off to play the last hole. Sure enough, Sluman's first shot hit the water, he made a double bogey, and missed the cut. Needless to say, Tony and Jeff wanted to kill me.

Several years ago, Robert Zielinski was staying with me. A good caddie friend of mine, Robert, was having no luck finding a job. He tried everything but nothing was falling into place. I was calling in every favor I could to try to get him a bag when suddenly I remembered I had "That Guy's" shaving kit at my place. As soon as Robert heard that, he told me to get rid of it. "Piddler," he said, "some things you just can't explain." We threw the shaving kit in the trash can, and in less than 10 seconds, the phone rang. Robert answered. It was Chip Beck on the other end, offering him a job.

If a player can't blame "That Guy" for his troubles, there is a long list of other excuses he can go with, for example; "My fingers feel fat today." "There was too much noise in my hotel room last night." "I should have switched putters." "I never should have had that hot dog." Players don't have to search too long to come up with something. The road to Hell is paved with good excuses. Every single player out on Tour has a stash of them. Everybody seems to be fine on the first tee. It's once they miss that first putt that excuses start to come. They start to stretch a little or twitch their shoulder. So then you ask, "Are you OK? Did you get hurt?" Then it comes. "Well, I was playing with the kids in the pool and I think I pulled something."

Dan and I celebrate eagle on the 18th at Waynesborough, a shot that won us the tournament.

Here's my theory on excuses: there's golf (which we all play), there's tournament golf (where they announce your name), and then there's Sunday tournament golf (where the guys with fewer excuses play). All the guys who didn't win on the weekend find the excuse that fits best.

Even for the best of the best, the excuse is always close at hand. I've seen Steve Williams (Tiger's caddie) take cameras from people more than once and throw them in the lake because the click may or may not have distracted Tiger during a shot. For the rest of us caddies, it's a hell of a lot easier. Our excuse for not winning is simply, "My player sucks!"

Here's a story you won't see on the Golf Channel. I've been to Europe a few times to work the British Open but there is one trip I will never forget, and it's not because we won. Things are a little different over there. The food and drink and jet lag can wreak havoc with your digestive system if you're not used to it, and everybody seems to travel by train. Those factors proved to be a lethal combination for caddie Rodney Wooller. We probably drank a little more than we should have on Wednesday night and that left Rodney with an upset stomach Thursday morning. We all hopped on the train that took us to the course but Rodney didn't make it the whole distance. He sharted (he thought it was just a fart but it wasn't) and it was running down his pants.

He got off at the next stop and bought the cheapest tracksuit package he could find. When he got back on the next train he went straight for the bathroom, took off his underwear and pants and threw them out the window. He quickly ripped open the package to put on his new tracksuit pants and realized why it was so cheap: there were no pants in the package. All he had purchased was a windbreaker. So he did what any person would do in that situation: he put his legs through the arms of the jacket and pulled the waistband up as high as he could. A caddie through and through, nothing was going to stop him from fulfilling the first part of the Caddie Credo, *Show up*. So, with his fancy track jacket covering as much skin as possible, he waddled right into the clubhouse like nothing was wrong. You've got to give it to the guy—he was pretty damn resourceful.

"I'm not much of a superstitious guy, but some of the caddies are. There was a guy who used to work for Loren Roberts, who we called Dirty Dan. One weekend they were in contention in the final group on Sunday in Milwaukee. There was a guy that worked in the caddie van—his nickname was the Black Cat and some of the other caddies referred to him simply as 'That Guy.' The reason he was working in the caddie wagon was that he could no longer get a bag. He missed 21 or 22 cuts in a row with Roger Maltbie. He wasn't a bad guy at all or even a bad caddie. He just never had any luck. So he's working in the kitchen and Dirty Dan walks in to have lunch before his 1:00 tee time with the final pairing. As soon as Dirty Dan saw who was working the caddie van, he turned around and walked out, drove back out the property, and redid the whole thing. He went and grabbed a hamburger outside the course and came in and started his day over again. Now, I'm not a superstitious guy, but it's hard to argue with what happened. Loren Roberts won the tournament and Dirty Dan picked up a pretty good paycheck.

The same type of thing happened to another caddie named Tony Navarro, who was working for Greg Norman at the time. Tony walked on a plane to go to the next tournament and saw 'That Guy' on it. He immediately walked off the plane and changed his flight to the next day. That's just how big of a black cat 'That Guy' was."

—RICK "RICK AT NITE" HIPPENSTIEL

Always stay away from 'That Guy'! Jeff Sluman was playing the first hole and he didn't have a coin to mark his ball so he borrowed a coin from him. Sure enough, he went on to shoot 83."

—"MINNESOTA" MIKE LEALOS

I cannot hand Bart [Bryant] the putter until we both have our feet on the green. It makes for extra work but I'll do whatever it takes to keep him happy and in his zone. Of course, I could just hand it to him and go do everything I need to do, put the bag down, clean the ball, and find tomorrow's pin placement. Instead I've got to walk him to the green, and only when we have our feet firmly on the green can I hand him his putter. It's not a big deal but it's a little peculiar."

—BOB "MR. CLEAN" CHANEY

"I worked for a guy that had this thing where every time he made a bogey he would take the ball out of play. I remember once we were on a tear where he'd birdied six in a row and then went on to bogey one. Sure enough, he told me to get rid of that ball. There was nothing wrong with that ball—in fact, I liked it. It was five under in the last seven holes and it was about to make me some serious money. I am also a little superstitious, so I really wanted him to keep playing with that ball. But I just couldn't talk him into keeping it."

—"ALASKAN" DAVE PATTERSON

"When Fred Couples first started out I'd always make sure that he had a 1967 quarter on him to mark the ball because 67 was the score he wanted to shoot every day."

—LINN "THE GROWLER" STRICKLER

"I was working for 'Crazy' Neal Lancaster. He has all the ability in the world, but he's just a waste of talent. After missing an eight-foot putt, he came up to me and said, in his North Carolina twang, **'God damn it, Dicky, you're a black cat. My ex-wife's a black cat, my girlfriend's a black cat, my caddie's a black cat. I got me a litter of black cats!'**"

—DICK "THE ANGEL" MARTIN

"I'm definitely superstitious. I never grab a pin sheet before I get to the first tee. I never put on my caddie bib before

I get to the first tee. I count the clubs at least 10 times from the time I meet my player in the morning to the time we get to the first tee. **I'm completely OCD, to the maximum extreme. Most people do something twice. I do it 10 times.** Also, I never put my hat or my visor on until I get to the first tee. Once I hit that first tee I have an awful lot to take care of."

–TOM ANDERSON

I'll wear the same hat until I miss a cut. When I miss the cut, I'll give it away to the first person I come across. Then I'll start with a new hat and continue to wear it until I miss another cut. Even if we play badly on the weekend, as long as that hat makes the cut it stays in. Sometimes that hat can get a little ripe. The fewer hats I use in a year the better I'm doing."

–ANTHONY WILDS

Players can be superstitious about lots of things, including their caddies. I had retired at the end of 2005 after a good run with Corey Pavin. Things had been going well but I was just getting sick of all of the travel. About a year later I was playing golf in 110-degree heat in Palm Springs when I got a call from Corey. I had read he'd missed the cut at the U.S. Open. He asked me if there would be any way I'd like to caddie again. I said sure, but I'd need to find the right player. (I wanted to mess with him a little.) 'To caddie for me you dumb f—' was his reply. We went to work on his putting and he started to put his game together again. He finished 21st in Hartford and then went on to win in Milwaukee."

–ERIC SCHWARZ

Carl Pettersson looks on as his caddie, Tommy Anderson, takes a snapshot of the Hogan Bridge during the Masters.

❝ I am superstitious but my superstitions don't seem to hold up. My superstitions only seem to work for part of the week and not for the rest. A couple of times I've found a penny head's up on the Sunday before the final round. I was sure it was a good sign that we'd win the tournament, but it wasn't, and we didn't."

—CHRIS "CRISPY" JONES

❝ I don't ever stand behind my player. I always need to face them, otherwise it will be a bad shot."

—DICK "THE ANGEL" MARTIN

❝ I never get the pin sheet before I go to the tee. And like most caddies, I hate to birdie the first hole of a tournament—unless, of course, we continue and birdie the second."

—DONNA EARLEY

❝ Leonard Thompson always needed to have the name on his bag facing toward the target—which was interesting because he was so severely dyslexic that he couldn't read it."

—JERRY "SKYSCRAPER" SCHNEIDER

❝ I keep track of the rounds that my shorts and my shirts score. I had a pair of shorts that I wore last year that were 50 over par for the year. (I should have gotten rid of them but they were really nice.) On the last day of Q-School, I thought that they were due for a good day—and sure enough they were. Brian Bateman played great and we made it through. I think I'll keep those shorts in the rotation for a while. I also have a shirt that I wear on Sundays. It has had a pretty good year so far—10 under par."

—JEFF "SKILLET" WILLET

Golf pros justify what they are doing by making sure missed shots are not their fault. It is a way for them to keep their confidence. They didn't hit a bad shot—it was a gust of wind that took the ball, or it took a bad bounce off the fairway. Some caddies will play into this, eagerly agreeing, 'That wasn't you, boss. There was mud on the ball, you hit it perfectly.'"

—GRAEME COURTS

I hate early calls on the ball. I get really upset if anybody throws out a call when my guy's putt is still rolling toward the hole. Early calls never work out. Just keep your damn mouth off my ball. I know it sounds like an excuse for missing shots, or a superstition, but it's actually a time-tested fact. (Although it does seem to work out for Tiger—sometimes.)"

—TOM JANIS

I can't have any garbage in the bag or in my pockets at any time because garbage produces garbage shots."

—JEFF DOLF

I used to think that if my player made a couple of putts while I was in the caddie crouch it had something to do with me. So I'd spend the rest of the day in that crouch while my guy was putting."

—JIM "BONES" MACKAY

"I won't go near a woman until the round is over. I won't even gamble near them. I avoid them like the plague. Women are bad luck, simple as that. When you see a woman on a bag you can add two strokes per day to that player's round."

—JOE "FREAK" BOSOWSKI

"Payne Stewart didn't want me to wash his golf ball. And it wasn't because I was black—he just wouldn't allow anyone but his own caddie to touch his ball."

—RICHARD "JELLY" HANSBERRY

"I will never, ever wear matching socks."

—"REEFER" RAY REAVIS

"Every year on Wednesday at TPC, the caddies get to take the shot on the par-3 17th over the water to the island green. It's a really cool thing for us and there always seems to be a story about it in the paper the next day. Most of the players throw some money in the pot for the caddie closest to the pin. John Daly (known for being the Tour's biggest tipper) is always the most generous and throws in at least a few hundred bucks. About 70 percent of the caddies hit it in the water. One year I was caddying for Doug Barron and I hit it dead right. It was an awful shot. It never had a chance of finding dry land. It went straight into the water. That Thursday we started on the back nine, and on our 8th hole (the 17th, with the island green) Barron put his shot right in the water and turned to me and said 'It's your fault, all I could think about was that awful shot you hit here yesterday.'"

—DICK "THE ANGEL" MARTIN

"A few years ago in Memphis we were playing with John Daly and Paul Azinger. On 14, Azinger missed a putt and raked his putter (took an air swing). It helicoptered in slow motion way up in the air and ended up in the pond. He went into the pond to get it and when he came out with it his putter—he uses that long putter—had green muck and goop hanging from it. We all stood at the back of the green cracking up."

—JEFF "SKILLET" WILLET

"I was in Milwaukee in 1987 and didn't get a job, so I was heading home. At the airport late that night I met Jim Thorpe and got a job as his caddie for the week. The next day he played the course blind and shot 65. We ended up finishing fourth. He asked me to caddie for him the following week and we went to the tournament in Flint where we finished fourth again. Then I stayed on his bag for the next tournament in Columbus, Georgia. By this time he's telling everybody what I great caddie I am. There was even an article in the paper about it. I was the guy who had turned his game around and now anything seemed possible. Anyway, we're down in Columbus and he has a wedge shot from about 85 yards. He hits it fat and lays a piece of sod over the ball, [leaving a divot] that's deep enough to bury a small puppy in. He looks at me and says, 'That was no goddamn 85 yards J.J.! Man, you can't count. You might be the worst caddie I've ever had on my bag.' I never worked for him again after that. Clearly, I was the problem.

"Another time I was up at a tournament in Canada where my buddy Golf Ball was working for Calvin Peete. Some people were being noisy, moving around and creating a distraction while Calvin was playing, so Golf Ball yelled out, 'Stand, please!' That's the universal crowd control term for 'stay still.' I guess the fans up in Canada weren't too familiar with golf because the entire gallery behind the green jumped to their feet.

"But a noisy crowd was nothing compared to the distraction Hal Sutton had to deal with when we were playing in Flint, Michigan. We were on the 17th hole par-3. Around that area, there was always a lot of action near the green, fans betting and tons of chatter. On the slope of the green, directly at the end of Hal's sight line for the putt was a young lady wearing a mini-skirt. She was sitting cross-legged and, wouldn't you know it, wearing absolutely nothing under her skirt. The other caddie, pro, and I all went over to 'help' Hal line up his putt. He had no idea why we were all standing behind him. 'Look up, Hal,' I said. 'Oh my God,' he replied, 'I've got no chance of making this putt.' He was right. He 3-putted."

—HILTON "J.J." JAMES

Golfers seldom hit a bad shot. Just ask them. It can be dead calm, and the pro could hit his shot a little fat and come up short. If an excuse doesn't come immediately to mind, wait for it. A minute later as you're walking up to the ball you'll feel a little wisp of wind and sure enough he'll say, 'I knew it was into the wind.'"

—JEFF KALEITA

Mud on the ball is always a good excuse. Players will use that one pretty fast."

—CHIP "ALABAMA" CARPENTER

I was in Milwaukee when a loud siren went off on the Tuesday of the tournament week. It was ear-shattering, like an air raid warning, yet not one single player on the range turned around to see what it was and no one stopped hitting balls. It was as if they were all robots hitting perfect shot after perfect shot. They weren't shaken at all. But as soon as the tournament started, every tiny thing was a crippling distraction."

—JOHN "DOC" ROMAN

"Some players will look to blame a poor shot on anything they can—the marshal raising the sign, the person moving in the background, a person with a mister (those tiny little fans that you can barely hear). When I was working for David Frost three years ago in Greensboro, he brought a 9-year-old kid to tears. Right when he was getting ready to take the club back for his swing, the kid hit the button on his mister. In the dead silence you could hear this hmmmmmmmmmmmm sound. David stopped, looked back in disgust and said, 'What are you doing?' In David's defense, he didn't know that it was a kid making the noise. But after that he didn't hit a very good shot, partly because he had to restart his routine and partly because he was feeling badly about what he'd done."

—TOM ANDERSON

"I've heard so many bullshit excuses on the course. The best excuse I've ever heard was from the club champion at Wanakah Country Club, which is set on the shores of Lake Erie, just south of Buffalo. A freighter was going by in the middle of the lake and caused the guy to miss a three-footer on the 14th hole. The freighter—a mile and a half away on the middle of Lake Erie—bothered him. He said it distracted him because it was in his line."

—CHUCK HART

"   The worst excuse I've heard for missing a shot is "I heard the scoreboard changing." Unless you're standing right under the damn thing it's impossible to hear the names and numbers changing. Silly answers like that are a sure sign the player is scrambling for excuses."

—TOM JANIS

"   Back in the '80s I was out at a bar celebrating a great week of golf with Roger Maltbie. We were at Quad Cities (a course he loved to play). He had just churned out a top-10 finish and was strutting around the bar with his $50,000 check from the PGA for his efforts. We got really banged up **and by the end of the night all I remember was Roger frantically looking for his check.** He couldn't find it anywhere and panic was beginning to set in. He was convinced that his wife was going to kill him. We looked everywhere but we weren't exactly seeing straight by that point of the night. The next morning, somebody from the bar called saying that the clean-up crew swept up his check. It didn't matter though because he'd already managed to have the PGA cut him a new one. The original is framed and still hanging in that bar."

—GREG "PIDDLER" MARTIN

"   Sometimes I think tournaments are won because both the player and the caddie are sharp, on the same page, and able to limit their mistakes. Other times I think it just comes down to luck. My good friend Jerry Woodard was caddying for the legendary Marilynn 'Mom' Smith. Things were going pretty well and she had just finished the front nine at one under par when Jerry realized that he'd been using the wrong pin sheet all along.

"Another time, Tommy Williams worked an entire round for Beth Solomon at the LPGA Championship using a yardage book for a completely different course."

—JERRY "SKYSCRAPER" SCHNEIDER

I've seen lots of strange things happen on the golf course, but none stranger than the time when we were playing in the U.S. Open qualifiers in Swiftly Heights. A fellow competitor hit his tee shot into the left rough and out of nowhere a beagle came running onto the course and picked up the golf ball in his mouth. We chased the dog all the way back to its house, but the tricky guy scurried under the fence and we couldn't get over it to get the golf ball back. The USGA official ruled it a lost ball, even though we could see the ball sitting in the yard. We just couldn't get in there to identify the ball as his. It was frustrating, to say the least. The official wouldn't let him take a drop so he had to go back and take a stroke."

—CHUCK HART

We were playing down in Hilton Head in '85 and we all had to come in from the course because we were told there was a fan roaming the course with a gun. Apparently, he was looking for Beth Daniel. There was an amateur playing in that tournament that looked a lot like Beth Daniel, so she put a sign on her hat that said *I'm not Beth Daniel.*"

—TOM THORPE

I was working the Westchester Open a few years back and the group in front of us had the big South African player Brenden Pappas. I noticed something strange going on between him and his caddie. The body language just wasn't right. By the time they got to the 7th hole, the caddie dropped the bag near the green and just walked off the course."

—JEFF "SKILLET" WILLET

"I like it when cops are coming down the cart path. I always tell them to stop and be still, even when my player really doesn't need to concentrate."

—HILTON "J.J." JAMES

"When you're traveling all over this country hustling to get from tournament to tournament, you never know what's going to happen. When we were playing down in Los Angeles, I rented a car. I pulled up to my hotel in Santa Monica and handed the keys to the valet parking guy. He gave me a claim ticket and I headed to the lobby to check in. Twenty minutes later I went back outside to get the car. I handed the ticket to another valet guy and he just gave me this blank stare. "I didn't park your car," he said. It turns out the car was stolen by a guy who looked an awful lot like a valet. The boys on the Tour had a good time ripping on me for that. I was called 'No Car-lucci' for quite a while."

—BILLY CARLUCCI

"One year we were playing Poppy Hills at the Pebble Beach Tournament. We were on the seventh tee waiting for the group in front of us to get out of the way. It was a cold and miserable day and there were hardly any people there. We noticed a guy coming toward us down the cart path on a bicycle. No big deal, we thought, just a guy probably heading home after the tournament. He was just coasting downhill and when he got closer to us one of the few spectators said, 'Hey, that's my bike!'

The guy ran right past us along the tee box and hit the rider with a forearm shiver that knocked him clear off the bike into a mud puddle. Just like that, the rightful owner hopped onto his bike and rode off."

—JIM "BONES" MACKAY

I have a reputation for saying what is on my mind. One week I was getting so frustrated with my player's inability to control her shots that I blurted out that she should 'Just hit the damn ball straight'. She proceeded to throw her club straight at my head. I threatened to take her over my knee and give her a good spanking. She told me to go f— myself. I responded by saying if I could do that, I wouldn't need bitches like her. We stayed together on tour for at least six more weeks. I think it was just her way of telling me she loved me."

—BILL "JUNKMAN" JENKINS

You want to know how stupid I am? I quit Curtis Strange. I quit him to go to Ben Crenshaw, who I'd always wanted to work for. But luck was not in my corner for that decision. Curtis went on to win two U.S. Opens while Crenshaw got a hyperactive thyroid and didn't make any money. He couldn't play for a while so I just jumped around to other players and ended up back with Curtis towards the end of his career on the regular Tour. Curtis still makes fun of me for that move. He never tires of telling me how much it cost me."

—JEFF "BOO" BURRELL

We were paired with Jim McMahon once during a pro-am and it was the strangest thing I'd ever seen. He played the whole round barefoot while drinking beer and smoking cigars. Eventually they made him put shoes on, but the drinking and the smoking couldn't be stopped."

—DONNA EARLEY

"We were playing Phoenix and there were three players in the group: Dan Forsman, Larry Mize, and Fulton Allem. Bullet—a very colorful character—was Fulton's caddie and, of course, Piddler was on Dan's bag. On the 4th hole par-3, Fulton hit his ball on the green. Bullet had to go the bathroom so he ran up ahead to the Sani-Hut on his way to the green. By the time my player and I made our way down the fairway, we saw Fulton and Bullet going at it. Turns out Bullet lost his yardage book somewhere. Fearing he'd lost it in the Sani-Hut he asked the scoring lady to do him a favor. 'Will you run up to the Sani-Hut and see if you can find the yardage book?' That was one big favor. She ran all the way back to it and didn't catch up with us until the next tee. Huffing and puffing, she told us that she couldn't find it. Somehow Bullet talked her into checking for it one more time so off she went, back to the portable john. By the next hole, she caught up to us again but this time she was holding a big wad of toilet paper. Turns out the yardage book had fallen into the toilet while Bullet was sitting on it, so armed with layers upon layers of paper around her hand, she reached in to get it. Fulton saw everything that was going on and he wasn't very happy about it. We finished the day with Fulton bogeying his last two holes. On the par three his shot went right into the bunker. He immediately held up his club, turned around, and yelled 'Bullet! What the Hell! I've got shit on my grips!' **That was it. We all just lost it. I didn't think we were going to make it back to the clubhouse, we were laughing so hard.**"

—CHUCK MOHR

"I was working for a 6'6", 270 pound long-driving pro named John McComish. We had a good week, making the cut and earning a $25,000 bonus for holing the 16th. Before taking off on Sunday afternoon he gave me my check for the week. When I looked at it later I noticed he was $1,000 light. I called him to let him know about his accounting error but he said it was no mistake. I wanted to kill him, but again, he was 6'6", 270 pounds, so instead I put a whammy on him and wished him a fiery death. You gotta remember, on Tour it's your wife, your kids, and your caddie...not necessarily in that order."

—BILL "JUNKMAN" JENKINS

"I used to have an old Volkswagen bus that a bunch of us would travel in. We'd have as many as 11 caddies in that thing, going from tournament to tournament. Once we were going from Hilton Head on the way to Atlanta when the engine blew. We got towed into some hillbilly place near Macon, Georgia, and none of us had the money to repair it. So we struck up a deal with the owners of the garage: **I sold them the van for a ride down to the tournament and three watermelons.**"

—JERRY "SPEEDWAY" AIKIN

"I've seen some good club throwing in my day. Once we were playing behind John Houston and I guess he didn't like one of his tee shots, so he threw his driver right into the middle of a water canal on the 3rd hole. When we got to the tee Houston was knee-deep in the water trying to find his driver. For the rest of the round, we could hear him with every step he took—squish-squish, squish-squish."

—JOHN "CHIEF" GRIFFIN

"I was working for Keith Fergus in Tucson and after our round we went to the chipping area at the far end of the driving range to work on a few things. The only thing near us was a metal maintenance shed. Every once in a while a ball from the driving range would hit the shed and it would make a loud noise. All of a sudden a ball made a really loud bang and rattled off the shed. **The next thing we know we're being attacked by bees. We started running like lunatics. I must have been stung at least 10 times. Keith went in one direction and I went in the other, and the bees all came with me. I just kept running and eventually made it to the lake off of the 18th hole. The tournament was still going on but I couldn't be stopped—I jumped right in and stayed in until I deemed it safe to get out.**"

—ARTIE GRANFIELD

"I was caddying for T.C. Chen, who was playing the Asian Tour during the months of February and March. We were at the Kuala Lumpur Open and there were monkeys swinging back and forth in the trees. I'd never seen anything like it before in my life. I was the only non-local caddie in the group and I was looking for a ball in the rough. The other caddies were also in there helping me but they each had a club in their hands. I wasn't sure why but I quickly understood when **all of a sudden a cobra popped up right in front of my face.** I ran like hell."

—"MINNESOTA" MIKE LEALOS

"Several years ago we were walking up to our ball on the 18th hole at Phoenix. We were waiting to hit our second shots while the group behind us hit their drives. The first drive hit our ball (which is a little annoying) then the guy right after him hit our ball again. Do you know what the odds of that happening are? **I doubt that has ever happened to anyone in the history of golf.**

"Another time, when I was working with Fuzzy Zoeller, he hit his ball toward the green but it hit a nearby tree. We looked all over the place for that ball and were about to give up and take a stroke when all of a sudden a little gust of wind came up. The ball fell out of the tree and right onto the fairway."

—JOHN "CADILLAC" CARPENTER

I was working for Scott McCarron and we were paired with Payne Stewart. It was a Friday and we were missing the cut badly. They both hit their drives and we were at least 40 to 50 yards ahead of Payne. As we were walking down the fairway **I asked, 'How far is that between those balls, Scott?' He chided, 'Well, there's enough room there to build a Wal-Mart.'** Payne Stewart stopped in his tracks, turned around to look at us and said, 'Well, boys, you better get busy or you're going to have all weekend to go shopping there.'"

—BOB "MR. CLEAN" CHANEY

I had a player ask me before his shot, 'What's the wind doing?' I told him that it was blowing into him from right to left. He looked at me and said 'How do you figure that?' I replied that all he had to do was look at the clouds. He answered, 'Well hell, I'm not going to hit it that high.'"

—"ALASKAN" DAVE PATTERSON

" Once we were playing an event down in Tampa, Florida, and we were on a hole with a pond to the right. Fred Couples was about eight yards from the pond. It was no big deal, he could just walk up to that ball and knock it on the green like he'd done thousands of times before. The only problem this time was that between the ball and the pond there was an alligator. It was at least an eight-footer and it was sunning itself on the bank. The people around us told us not to worry, that if they aren't provoked nothing will happen. In fact, they said that if you walk towards 'gators, they normally go into the water. But I grew up in Connecticut, so what do I know? And I didn't particularly like the word 'normally' being used. **There was nothing 'normal' about this situation.**

"Fred looked at me and said 'Joe, you have to get that 'gator in the water, otherwise there's no way I'll be able to hit this shot.' I thought he was kidding. He wasn't. Now, there are lots of things that I'll do for my player, but chasing an alligator wasn't one of them. I told Fred I was sorry, but I just wasn't prepared to take one for the team like that. I did let him know that he had the option of taking an unplayable. Anyhow, Fred eventually walked toward it, and it didn't go back into the water—it just sat there and watched the shot. I guess it didn't bother Fred that much because he shot it and put the ball within 12 feet of the hole, without any help from me."

—JOE LaCAVA

" My Cadillac was stolen and stripped while I was working a tournament in L.A. The cops found it and told me it was 'drivable.' All that I knew was that I had to get to Phoenix for the next tournament because I was working for a good player. I'm not exactly sure what the cops meant by 'drivable' because the car had nothing left in it. I mean *nothing*. It didn't even have windows. I had to buy a beach chair and strap myself in for the long drive to Phoenix. When I eventually got there and pulled into the parking lot the guys just started laughing their asses off. Luckily for me, one of my buddies didn't get a bag that weekend so he took it to the junkyard and furnished it with everything it needed. **L.A. to Phoenix in a beach chair. I promised my player I'd get there!**"

—ARTIE GRANFIELD

"   My friend 'Handlebar' Rick had a chance to go on Tour with Hale Irwin but he turned him down. I remember him saying 'Ah, that guy's nothing more than a football player. He'll never make it.' Handlebar could have retired on that bag."

—BOB "MR. CLEAN" CHANEY

"   I am probably the least successful caddie there has ever been. In the last 29 years I've averaged a top-10 finish once every two years. If you haven't found your horse out on the Tour after nearly three decades you probably never will. So **you absolutely need to be out here for the love of the game, and you need to get creative in finding ways to make a little cash to survive**. Once I was sitting in the caddie tent without a job because my player had missed the cut. From where I was sitting, I could see people driving in looking for places to park their cars. So I made up a little sign that said 'Parking Here $3.00,' and started parking cars in a yard that was near the golf course. After parking about nine or 10 cars, this guy walks out of his house and starts yelling at me, 'What the hell are you doing in my yard?' If he had a shotgun he would have blown me away. I disappeared as fast as I could."

—JERRY "SPEEDWAY" AIKIN

Bones McKay and Phil Mickelson celebrate their win at the 2005 PGA Championship.

“ Fluff Cowan was caddying for Peter Jacobsen and they were on the last green at St. Andrews. Peter saw a streaker preparing to run onto the green and told Fluff that he was going to take the guy out. Fluff replied that he should just concentrate on his putt and finish the tournament. Jacobsen protested that it was what his high school football career was for. Sure enough, as the streaker did his second lap around the green—and before security could do anything about it—Jacobsen lined up his angle of attack, took off in hot pursuit, and absolutely nailed him. Jacobsen said later that as he tackled him he had to turn his head to avoid getting a mouthful."

—GRAEME COURTS

SIX

CADDIE KNOWS BEST

I've been on the Tour for a very long time. After all these years, a little wisdom was bound to sink in. At the end of it all, my advice boils down to simply this: know your surroundings. This goes for players and caddies alike.

A long time ago I was working for Dennis Trixler in Mississippi. We were playing with Mitch Adcock. Both Dennis and Mitch were sponsored by Titleist and used the same equipment. We were on the 4th hole par-3, 184 yards to the pin. Trixler asked me for my advice. 'It's a 7 iron,' I said, 'but you need to hit it hard.' 'No, it's a 6 iron,' he said. 'All right, you're the boss.' So he took out the six iron and hit it well over the green. As walked up to the ball he asked me, 'Why didn't you tell me to hit that 7 iron?' 'Dennis, I did.' 'Well," he responds, 'you weren't firm enough with me.' He proceeded to chip it up on the green with a putt to save his par. He missed the short putt and then he was really pissed off. He walks over with his putter in hand and starts beating the shit out of his bag. I mean, he's really mad and he's giving it to this poor bag. He's hitting it with the club, he's kicking it with his cleats, he knocks it over and continues to pound on it. He literally rips this bag to shreds. Suddenly he stops. I figured he'd gotten all of his aggression out and was ready to move on. Nope. All of a sudden he realized he'd been beating the wrong bag. It was Adcock's Titleist bag that was lying there in pieces. No problem for me though. I had to carry Trixler's bag for the next 14 holes while the other caddie was stuck carrying Adcock's bag for the rest of the day with both arms wrapped around it so his clubs, balls and tees wouldn't fall out.

So, my advice is if you're gonna kick a bag make sure it's your own, or from a caddie's perspective, never let your player destroy his own bag. Either way, it comes down to knowing your surroundings.

FOR THE PLAYERS:

Golf is always history. Once you do it, it's finished. You win a tournament or a championship and by the next week it's history and there's another tournament starting. If you miss a shot on the golf course you have to go find that little white ball and hit it again. You're always moving forward but sometimes your head won't let you. If you can think about the present and not be in the past you'll have a pretty good day on the golf course."

—HILTON "J.J." JAMES

Don't spend as much time on the range as you do on the short game area. Learning to chip and putt will be much more helpful in shaving strokes off your game."

—CHUCK HART

"   Don't let the golf course beat you. If you're in trouble, punch out and give yourself a chance to putt for a par. Don't allow the double bogey to come into play."

—"REEFER" RAY REAVIS

"   I truly believe that a young player coming out on Tour would benefit greatly from having an experienced caddie on his bag. A lot of guys go out with a friend as a caddie, but because of the way things are with tournament eligibility, new players need to make money and earn points every time they go out. They don't have time to experiment; they need to go out there and produce. An experienced caddie would definitely save them some shots."

—JOHN "CADILLAC" CARPENTER

"   Less grip pressure! When they get over the ball, so many people just want to kill it. When we do the pro-ams, the professional athletes are always guilty of this—especially the football players. As soon as you lessen your grip pressure you become less tense and you are able to swing so much better."

—DONNA EARLEY

"   If you can putt, you'll make money."

—ARTIE GRANFIELD

"   Pay attention to what everybody else's balls are doing on the green. Don't focus so much on what your shot is going to do. You can figure it out by studying what the other balls are doing—especially when it comes to speed—no matter what your line is."

—TOM JANIS

A tip for the amateur: swing within yourself. **The biggest mistake I see is amateurs swinging too hard.** Believe me, you'll hit it farther by hitting it better. It will always go farther well struck than it will when swung at hard and miss-hit."

—ANTHONY WILDS

The biggest mistake I see the amateurs making out there is hitting with too little club. They think they can hit a seven iron 160 yards like the pros do and it really goes 145 and it always comes up short. That's the biggest thing. **Almost all amateurs are guilty of not hitting the ball as far as they think they will.** They're also totally unaware of good course management. To them, par-5 means if they get a good drive, then they're going to hit a 3 wood no matter what. They might be leaving themselves a 40-yard shot with the pin over a bunker downwind, which is tough. You'd be better off hitting a driver and then figuring out a 6 iron 90-yard and then hit a full sand wedge and have it spin. They all think they hit it further than they do."

—AL MELAN

I've been around some golfers who are really volatile. They just don't enjoy themselves out there and it's a labor for them. They're so miserable when they play golf. But you know what? It's never that bad. We're out here playing golf. That's a pretty good job to have and **the golf course is a pretty nice office. It sure beats a cubicle.**

"It's only a game—how bad can it be? I think I've enjoyed my life more by seeing some miserable millionaires out there. It's made me appreciate what I have. I know it's tough to play at that level, but come on! Get some perspective.

"If you're looking to shave some strokes off your game, the most important thing all players should remember is to practice their short game. These guys all hit long, but they separate themselves with their short game. If you're a decent putter and a decent chipper, you're always going to be able to play and enjoy your golf. Practice and try to develop some kind of feel. Enjoy the game. And remember, it's only a game."

—MARK CHANEY

The worst thing a pro golfer can do is bring his wife to a tournament. In 1972, I was at a tournament caddying for Sam Snead. He walked up to one of the bright, up-and-coming players and said, 'You came here to work at one of the hardest mental sports in the world. You need everything you've got to compete. If you think you can bring your wife out here *and* keep her happy and play well, you're crazy.' The next day, that young player sent his wife home and within three months he was excelling on the Tour."

—JOE "FREAK" BOSOWSKI

A lot of the amateurs take this game way too seriously. We do pro-ams every Wednesday and a lot of the time those guys are out there trying to beat the pros. They're good players, but they're playing on tees that are 30 to 60 yards in front of the pro on every hole. Most of the time my player doesn't play well on Wednesdays. The amateurs will approach me and say, 'Man, he's really struggling out there.' Then the next day he'll go out there and shoot a 68 and I'll just chuckle to myself. A

6 iron that goes 183 on Wednesday can go 196 on Thursday because of all the adrenaline coursing through his body. That's when the pros really come out to play."

—TOM ANDERSON

Don't try to kill it. Don't think you're better than you are."

—JEFF "BOO" BURRELL

The worst thing about this sport is that we only turn our heads to the left. All day long, with every putt we hit, every swing we make, we look to the left three or four times on every shot (factoring in the practice swings and pre-putt rituals). You do that for a lifetime and those muscles on the left side of your neck are going to get much stronger than those on your right. A golfer is constantly pulling across himself with his left chest or pectoral muscles, so he gets overdeveloped on the left side of his chest compared to his right. Then on his right, the muscles in his back are overdeveloped so they get twisted up.

"My best tip for a golfer is to buy heavily weighted clubs and swing them with the opposite hand until the non-golf muscles catch up to the golf muscles. I've seen a lot of golfers make the mistake of going on a weight-training program and they put more strength on what's already imbalanced. Then a stronger imbalance turns into stronger tension and major back problems. Plenty of golfers have suffered back injuries and been forced to pull out of events or miss them completely because of this injury. Don't make that mistake."

—JOHN "DOC" ROMAN

Swing within yourself. In the last 16 years we haven't played with more than 10 amateur golfers who have played to their handicap. The greens are always faster and the rough is thicker than they're used to. They get nervous playing with us and they try to hit shots they've never hit before. **I always end up telling these guys they have LOFT: Lack of F—ing Talent!** My best advice to them is to find the beer cart and have a couple so they'll be more relaxed and sure to play better."

—BRIAN LIETZKE

So often golf comes down to the short game. A lot of amateurs can't get it on the green from 30 yards. Working on chipping and putting will help anyone have more fun playing golf regardless of his ability."

—DALE MCELYEA

Take more club than you think you should hit. I see it every week at the pro-ams—the amateurs never take enough."

—CHRIS "CRISPY" JONES

Don't overthink the game. Just relax. Back when I worked for Larry Mize in the '90s, we won a couple of tournaments and we got invited to that big Johnnie Walker World Championship of Golf down in Jamaica. It was basically the top 30 players in the world. Larry got picked because he had such a big year and won a couple tournaments. Larry, a real family man, called me up and said, 'This tournament's a week before Christmas and the kids have got a lot of plays and pageants and other activities going on. I don't really want to be in Jamaica, but my wife says she'll take care of everything and that I should just go ahead and play.' Jamaica in December sounded all right to me. 'OK, let's go,' I agreed. But he put in a disclaimer: 'I'll tell you one thing though, I haven't unpacked my clubs since I got back from Japan a couple weeks ago. We're just going to go down there to have a good time, sign four score cards, and come home.' He won the tournament by 10. He shot 18 under par and I think Fred Couples was the next closest with eight under. I think his wife was pretty happy she made him go."

—CHUCK MOHR

Don't take things too seriously. You have to understand the game. Tiger Woods is the best player in the world and he can't do it perfectly every day. So try to keep that in perspective."

—BOB "MR. CLEAN" CHENEY

Remember, there are no trees in the middle of the fairway."

—BILL "JUNKMAN" JENKINS

There is something that I see in all the pro-ams and at least 90 percent of the amateurs are guilty of it. When they hit a ball in the rough and it isn't very far off the tee—still a couple hundred yards from the green—they'll march in there with a wood because they're still so far from the green. What they should be doing is taking a 9 iron or a pitching wedge in there and knocking it out a hundred yards down the fairway. You see it all the time. It's amazing how often you see it. Of course, they're lucky if they even hit the ball. They're lucky if it even goes 10 yards. Usually, it only goes five, and instead of chasing a par or a bogey they make a triple bogey or worse."

—CHUCK MOHR

"The very least a player can do is put on a good show on the weekends. That's when Mom is watching you on TV. Don't embarrass her."

—LINN "THE GROWLER" STRICKLER

"Don't waste your time playing in those Monday pro-ams chasing after $1,000 purses. Take Monday off, play Tuesday, and practice Wednesday. One tournament win gets you a couple years of gravy. A win on Tour gets you into the Mercedes and the World Golf Championship at the start of every year, and that's guaranteed money. Also, remember not to think too much. The guys that are book smart tend to have paralysis by analysis. The guys that are able to stop overthinking and just allow themselves to be are the ones who have the most success."

—JEFF "SKILLET" WILLET

"The biggest mistake that amateurs make is trying to make shots they have no business attempting. When you make a bad shot, just get the thing back in play and take your bogey instead of trying the impossible and taking a triple bogey or worse."

—JIM "SPRINGBOARD" SPRINGER

"Conquer the wedge! I would work on every shot from 100 yards in. Forget about the Big Bertha or whatever hybrid you think will hit your ball farther."

—JERRY "SPEEDWAY" AIKIN

"These guys don't just play, they play *tournament* golf. It's a four-day marathon, not an 18-hole sprint. And it's not a one-tournament deal, it's a 30-tournament deal. The ones that do well, like the top-40 players, just want to give themselves a chance to play everyday. They know that they'll have their good weeks, but they just want to give themselves the best opportunity to succeed every week, to make all the cuts and to be there on Sunday."

—"MINNESOTA" MIKE LEALOS

FOR THE PGA TOUR

The PGA does not allow the caddies in the clubhouse and that's something that might never change. We got sick of waiting to be allowed in so we went ahead and got our own clubhouse. It's a clubhouse on wheels. We call it the Caddie Wagon and it is easily the best thing that the PGA has ever done for us. To be honest, it never would have been possible without the help of the players on Tour, especially Carl Pettersson and Davis Love. Both of those guys went to bat for us with the commissioner, and the end result was a sanctuary on wheels that's worth well over a million dollars. The thing is unbelievable; we get anything we want from it (at seriously reduced prices). It is equipped with satellite TV (usually on the Golf Channel). We have five big flat screens, a computer, Internet access, and most importantly, it's a place we can call home.

"But it's not just the caddies that hang out in the Wagon. Every morning you can count on Phil Mickelson, Sergio Garcia, Rocco Mediate and others to stop by for breakfast. Onboard you'll find everything a caddie needs to survive: food, drinks, cigarettes, suntan lotion, bug spray, Tylenol, Advil, Aspirin.... Donna and Bob Schulz cook and take care of things on the Wagon and our PCTA president Dale McElyea runs the entire operation. The Caddie Wagon travels to 26 events throughout the year.

"There is one slight catch—from Monday to Wednesday we share the Wagon with all the golf reps that go from event to event. By Wednesday they all clear out, and whenever we need balls or clubs for ourselves or for friends those guys are very generous. Even if we have a few gripes with the PGA, it certainly isn't all that bad. By the way, Donna makes the most amazing banana pudding and when word spreads around that she's made some, both players and caddies come around as fast as they can. It's usually gone within an hour."

—GREG "PIDDLER" MARTIN

The Tour needs to look after the older caddies and provide them with the opportunity to get a job as a caddie master or another job at a club. The PGA has so much money and power but there are guys who have been out there for 20 or 30 years with nothing to show for it. The PGA could really do something good for those guys, even if it was just hooking them up with a 'retirement'-type job at a club."

—DICK "THE ANGEL" MARTIN

Our lives would be so much better and easier if we were allowed to have access to the clubhouse."

—CHRIS "CRISPY" JONES

I would change the way the money is distributed. It's too top heavy—the purses have gotten outrageous. Only the players that make the cut get money but all of the players and caddies have the same expenses. If you took just one of today's $1 million first-place payouts, it would still be more than the

Joey Damiano and Stuart Appleby talk strategy at the Masters.

combined career totals of Sam Snead, Byron Nelson, and Ben Hogan. That's why the Senior Tour is so great—there is no cut."

—BRIAN LIETZKE

There are all kinds of rules that I'd like to change. But I would love to work out a better way to deal with slow play. It's a very big problem out on Tour. Currently, the Tour tries to deal with it by fining players for slow play, but the money to these guys doesn't mean anything. What they need to do is start hitting them with strokes. When their scores go up and they miss cuts, *then* the money might mean something to them. I think if they started to penalize the players with shots, the slow play would go away."

—JOEY DAMIANO

It always bothers me that when you land in a divot in the middle of a fairway, you don't get a drop. You really should be allowed to move that ball out of the divot. You should not be penalized for hitting your ball in the fairway."

—"REEFER" RAY REAVIS

I hate it when the player is addressing the ball and the caddies stand behind the player to help them line up their shot. This is especially the case on the Ladies Tour. It takes too much time and slows up the game. It's unnecessary and I'd outlaw it. I doubt Ben Hogan ever had somebody line him up before his shot."

—JERRY "SPEEDWAY" AIKIN

We're still not allowed in the clubhouse. The PGA is the only tour in the world with that rule. In Japan, Australia, Europe, even at the British Open, the caddies have access to the clubhouse. You can go in there during rain delays and dry the clubs off. You can do anything that you have to do to get the bag ready. You cannot do that on this tour. Period. To be honest, we don't really care about being in the clubhouse—we just don't have anywhere to go to the bathroom. When you've got a morning tee time and you've got other things to do and you have to go to the stinky old Sani-Hut, that's just the worst way to start the day."

—CHUCK MOHR

Things have definitely gotten better for the caddies in the 20 years that I've been out here. I remember when I first started out looking up to Bruce Edwards. He and his player Tom Watson were always doing things for the right reasons and I respected both of them immensely. Bruce was constantly looking out for the caddies and wanting to change things for the better. I (along with several other veteran caddies) am trying to continue that legacy by working for the guys coming down the road. I'm trying to get insurance and some sort of retirement package for the guys. It's proving to be really hard to get it done. I just keep butting heads with the Tour. I wish that the powers that be were a little more responsive."

—JOE LaCAVA

The older golf courses are the best. The new ones are long with wide fairways and a lot of bunkering. They just don't have much character to them. To make the game harder, you shouldn't go longer and wider. You should go tighter. Some of the best holes are at Colonial, where it is tight and tree-lined, and at the Memorial, where it is wide with deep rough. It's amazing how, when there's a good amount of rough, these guys don't hit it as straight as they usually do. And, of course, the Wachovia Championship in Charlotte, North Carolina, is on the A-list. It has some goofy holes, but it's got the length. It's tight enough and it's got plenty of rough. It's not just smash and bash, which is how a lot of these young guys play. **Shot making is a lot less than what it used to be.**"

—BILLY CARLUCCI

I would like to wind the clock back to a time when we used golf balls that wouldn't go straight if they were miss-hit. I think the long hitters today hit their drivers everywhere and it doesn't matter that much where the ball goes. If it's a 450-yard hole and you can drive it 330 yards you only have a wedge to get to the green. It doesn't matter as much if you're in the rough, the sand, or in the fairway."

—GRAEME COURTS

I don't think the players get treated well enough. When we go out to do a Monday practice round they don't have water out on the golf course or snacks at 10:00 and 1:00. If it were Michael Jordan walking out there I bet they'd have it. These are professional athletes and they should be taken care of."

—BOB "MR. CLEAN" CHANEY

Anybody who wins on the U.S. tour should automatically be allowed to play in the Masters. In the old days, getting into Augusta was the reason players came to play on the U.S. tour in the first place. Fortunately that rule was reinstated, and I hope it stays that way."

—JOHN "CADILLAC" CARPENTER

It is ridiculous how far the balls go these days. The game has changed because of it. **When I was growing up, I was taught to hit it down the fairway. That's not so important anymore. Now you just need to know how to hit it hard.** A premium is placed on getting it as far down there as possible, even if it's in the rough. You can get your ball closer to the pin out of the rough with a wedge than with a five iron out in the fairway. Now players hit the ball almost 400 yards. Changes to the balls and the drivers have had a big impact on the game. But, somewhere down the line, you've go to stop it. You've got to govern the equipment companies and say, 'This is enough.'"

—FRED BURNS

I feel like some of the rules need to be more clearly stated. I've seen Piddler get two guys disqualified (which is not an easy thing for a caddie to do) for rule violations that were very vague. I've done it myself, inadvertently. A while ago I got my boss penalized with a couple shots in Akron, Ohio, for picking up a moving ball during the drop. I'm not exaggerating when I say that we had a really good chance to win the tournament if it wasn't for my error. I picked the ball up on the first drop, knowing that he was going to drop it again. The ball was rolling down this cart path, so I just picked it up instead of chasing it down. It went far enough, as far as I was concerned. I don't know if I got screwed or not, but I don't feel like I was in the wrong. The ball is supposed to roll two club lengths—I thought it did; the rules guy said it didn't. He didn't call the penalty until two holes later. I just had to accept what happened.

"Stuart Appleby wasn't very happy with me and he didn't talk to me for two weeks after that episode. I'd call him, he wouldn't answer. I'd text him, saying 'I accept my fate. I'll do whatever you want me to do.' No answer. Finally, he sent me an e-mail saying everything was cool. I just felt awful about the whole situation. It's not even about the lost money or the possibility of winning the tournament—he's my friend and I felt like I messed things up for him. I would have felt better about it had I known that I committed a clear foul, but as far as I was concerned I hadn't. The rules need to be more clearly laid out, it's as simple as that. I've seen plenty of guys do the same thing I did and with no penalty assessed. It shouldn't just be left to the discretion of the rules official who happens to be on the scene."

—JOEY DAMIANO

We should be allowed into the clubhouse and it should be an open bar."

—DALE MCELYEA

Caddies don't care about the recognition. All we need is a little respect. It's just the little things, like coming to a tournament and having a decent place to park. The PGA established the rule that players on tour must come with a caddie and for years we have had to park 10 miles away with the public (and the players) parked in a way better spot. For the longest time we didn't even have a place to go to escape bad weather. All of those things are starting to change.

"Do I need my name on TV? No. Do I need to be highlighted in a book? No, I don't need any of those things. But I do think we deserve a little respect to make my job easier—being able to get to work without a hassle, having a place to duck into when electrical storms hit, things like that."

—AL MELAN

The pro-ams are a drag. You end up playing with guys who sucked up to their bosses at their corporate jobs so that they could be out on the course with the pros. They think they know what they're doing but they don't. They're playing with a bunch of golf balls that click like false teeth. Unless you get the true CEOs, who are great people and extremely generous, you end up with a bunch of rude assholes who don't tip much."

—JOE "FREAK" BOSOWSKI

66 They're making courses so that they play right into the hands of the long ball hitters. Once we were paired with Mickelson and he was consistently hitting the ball 60 to 80 yards past Corey Pavin's ball. Phil would take out a wedge for his second shot and we'd be using a 5-iron. I just wish that instead of making the courses longer, they'd tighten the fairways a little, get the rough up longer and harden the greens. Then we'd see some good skill golf."

—ERIC SCHWARZ

66 I'd get rid of the discrimination against the caddies. It used to be ridiculous—**we had to get our yardage books from the pro-shops—but we weren't even *allowed* into the pro-shops.** Things have gotten a little better, but the discrimination is still there."

—JOHN "CHIEF" GRIFFIN

66 I would change the out-of-bounds rule. I just don't think it's right that when you hit one shot out of bounds you get a 2-stroke penalty. I think that's terrible. I would change the penalty to one shot."

—JEFF "BOO" BURRELL

66 It's only been recently that the PGA started doing anything for the caddies. They have thrown us a bit of a bone as far as medical coverage is concerned. They're giving every caddie $1,000 a year toward medical insurance if you have it. I pay $730 a month, so that thousand dollars isn't going very far, but at least it's a start. What I would really love to get going is some sort of retirement plan. The PGA is able to raise a lot of

money for charities. With high-profile sponsors that have deep pockets and its lucrative TV deals, the PGA has a lot of money to help. The players have a great retirement deal and, in all fairness, I understand that the tour exists because of the players, not because of the caddies. I understand that we're small fish swimming in the shark pool, but because of the simple fact that rules state that all players must have a caddie, the events need us. We could certainly use some help from the Tour."

—Al Melan

"I would make a change so that everybody would play every match at the Ryder Cup. Guys work so hard to get on the Ryder Cup teams. I just don't think it's fair that once they finally get there, they could potentially have to sit out."

—Jim "Bones" Mackay

"The Tour does not like caddies. **The PGA Tour is the only one where the caddies are not allowed in the clubhouse.** It doesn't happen in Europe and it doesn't happen in Asia. It's embarrassing, really. It would also be great if the PGA shared some of its bib money with us. The caddies are required to wear the sponsor bib which takes in an average of $500,000 each week for the Tour, but the caddies receive nothing for it. We could alleviate all caddie health, pension, and insurance problems simply by giving the caddies fair market value for wearing that bib everyday. I am sick and tired of hearing about old famous caddies who die in nursing homes completely destitute."

—Anthony Wilds

"**We have to figure out a way to get the caddies health insurance.**"

—Artie Granfield

"I would change the way we do the pro-ams. We should play nine holes with one group, then play the next nine with another. Sometimes the pro-ams can drag on. You can play with a great group or you can end up with people with big egos who get upset when the player outdrives them. At least by splitting it up a little the end would always be in sight."

—DONNA EARLEY

"I would require that all the players use exactly the same ball. Think about it: golf is the only sport where you get to choose your own ball, and the science is so great with the balls now that they can be tailor made to suit a player's game. Having the same ball would make things more consistent."

—LINN "THE GROWLER" STRICKLER

"The first thing I would change about the Tour would be caddie parking. They always have us so damn far away. We walk all day long on the golf course. I just don't see the need to walk a couple more miles to my car."

—"REEFER" RAY REAVIS

"To be honest, I really don't care about not being allowed in the clubhouse. Sure, it might make things a little easier, but I would much rather be hanging out with the guys in the Caddie Wagon."

—JERRY "SKYSCRAPER" SCHNEIDER

"I'm just happy we're allowed to wear shorts now. Those first 25 years of wearing long pants in 100-degree heat were a killer."

—"ALASKAN" DAVE PATTERSON

SEVEN

THE HALL OF SHAME
AND THE HALL OF FAME

CADDIE CREDO #7:
*"A golfer can erase the memory of a bad shot with a great one,
but a caddie never forgets."*

As in all sports, mistakes happen. In golf, players make mistakes
and it might cost them a stroke or two, then they can go on to
make an unforgettable shot that will easily replace any mistakes
they might have made during the round. With caddies it can
be a little different. When a mistake is made, it can result in a
disqualification and ruin both your and your player's chances of
a big paycheck, which can then affect your player's ranking and
his chances of getting into other tournaments. Of course, once
that happens he can kiss any lucrative endorsements goodbye.
This is probably why most players don't have much tolerance
when it comes to missteps from their caddies and why caddies
have been fired with such frequency in the past. I was lucky
that Dan Forsman looked past my ball-dropping debacle at Bay
Hill that got both him and Quigley disqualified on a Sunday,

and I am equally as fortunate to still be around after Dan and Don Pooley were disqualified for playing the wrong ball for four holes. (However, I still claim innocence on that one.)

Here's what happened. We were playing the Pleasant Valley Country Club in Worcester, Massachusetts. We were on that really historic par-4 15th hole, where in those days you'd hit a 2 iron off the tee and then you'd walk through that great covered bridge to get to your ball. The second shot is blind because the green is up high and you can't even see the flag so the guys hit a 9 iron or a wedge. The weather was miserable, it was raining like a son of a bitch and as you know we play through all that. (The only thing that suspends play is a flood or lightning.) I was standing next to my buddy Rick "Rick at Nite" Hippenstiel, who was caddying for Don Pooley, and we were under the umbrellas with the clubs. Both Dan and Pooley put their second shots on the green and walked up to their balls. Nobody was around because the weather was so brutal. Now, normally the player will pick up his ball and flick it to the caddie, who will wipe it off and give it back to his pro, then the pro will putt it out. This time, though, because the rain was coming down so hard, both players picked up their balls, wiped them off on their shirts and then went ahead and putted. Pooley made his for birdie and Dan two-putted for par, but it turns out they putted one another's balls.

The next hole was a par-3 and the players just kept their balls as they walked to the tee. Neither Rick nor I saw the balls to see that they were playing the wrong ones. At this point, my only job was to hold the umbrella. Should the players have looked at their balls to make sure they were playing the right ones? Maybe. But that didn't happen. They both parred the 16th and we continued on to the 17th hole. I was doing my best to keep things dry for Dan and he was rolling along. Both players made par at 17, which was great, considering the weather. Dan hit first on the par-5 18th and pushed his tee shot into the woods. Pooley put his right down the middle of the fairway. We managed to find our ball in the woods and when we got there Dan said that it wasn't his. 'The hell it isn't,' I answered. The official who happened to be there just scratched his head and said repeatedly, 'God damn' and 'I haven't seen *this* before.' So then Pooley came over to see what the commotion was about and looked down at the ball and said 'Golly, that's *my* ball!' Oops. Now, what's really interesting is that Pooley was playing a different ball that had come from his bag and Dan's ball had ended up in Pooley's bag. Did my buddy Rick not realize that Dan was playing the wrong ball, or was he just trying to cover for Pooley? Regardless, both players were immediately disqualified and, as usual, the caddies were left to take the blame.

    The worst shot I ever had the pleasure to see was a tee shot from the 9th hole at TPC in 1991. David Peoples whiffed the ball off the tee box. The ball dribbled across the cart path and into the flower garden right off the tee. **The shot probably didn't go more than 30 yards. But I didn't laugh—that flower garden was costing me money."**

—ANTHONY WILDS

    I was working for Woody Blackburn in New Orleans. We were paired with Tom Watson and his caddie, Bruce Edwards. We were on the 15th hole, which was a straightaway 3 wood lay-up followed by a 7 or 8 iron to the green. Woody hit the 3 wood off the tee and I'm not kidding when I say this ball started 80 yards off line. It went straight into a huge lake that ran along the 14th green. Woody looked at me and with desperation in his voice, asked, 'You think it might've got across the water?' Bruce and I just couldn't help it, we laughed so hard."

—JERRY "SKYSCRAPER" SCHNEIDER

"At the U.S. Open at Bellerive Country Club in St. Louis, Tom Kite hit it so far off the heel of the club that it hit a guy in the gallery who was not 10 yards in front of him on the left side of the tee. It hit him right in the leg. It was a one-hopper. If it had been anymore on the neck, it would have gone through Tom's legs. It was actually on TV. The world saw it. He was very apologetic. He thought he had hurt the guy."

—CHUCK HART

"We were playing at the original home of the Honda Classic and I was working for Isao Aoki. It was his third shot on a par-5 and he shanked it right into the woods. He looked at me and said 'Oh, J.J., never shank' and kept mumbling in Japanese as he walked into the bushes. If I had been standing a foot farther forward he would have hit me, it was so bad. But he managed to punch it out onto the green and made a long putt to save par."

—HILTON "J.J." JAMES

"I was working for Mark Wiebe at the Atlanta Country Club and he had a wedge in his hands and about 70 yards to the hole. I was thinking birdie when all of a sudden the ball comes flying right by my face and straight out of bounds. It was a stone shank. **It was the most sideways thing I'd ever seen in my life.** Mark just put his hands on his hips and said, 'What the hell was that?'"

—ARTIE GRANFIELD

"I was on the green with Gavin Coles at the Deutsche Bank Championship in Boston. On the second day, we were a couple under par and things were going pretty well—until he 4-putted from three feet. He hit it back and forth, back and forth, and when he got to his fourth putt (still with three feet left), he said, 'Should I try to make it or should I just run it up close so I can get the next one in?'"

—JEFF KALEITA

A few years ago I was working for Lorena Ochoa and we were on the 10th hole in Atlanta. She left her putt on the edge of the cup. She casually went up to tap it in and she whiffed it. I think we were both in shock."

—TOM THORPE

Years ago Fred Funk's wife sent out a letter to all the other wives saying that caddies were making too much money. Fortunately all the players threw that letter away."

—BOB "MR. CLEAN" CHANEY

Anyone who has ever been to Spyglass in California will realize how bad this shot was. On the 1st hole, there is just absolutely no way you can knock your shot out of bounds, no matter how badly you hit it, but Billy Ray Brown actually hit it out of bounds—off the tee. (Hopefully he's able to laugh about it now.) There's a tree about 20 yards away and he hooked the ball so badly that it hit the tree and went across the road. If you had asked anybody who knows the course if it is possible to knock it out of bounds on number one, everybody would say no. But Billy Ray proved that it is possible. He was playing so badly back then, he couldn't break 80. I felt bad for him because he really is a great guy."

—JEFF "BOO" BURRELL

"I was working for Scott McCarron and I had given him the yardages and pulled the club. While he was getting ready to hit I went ahead and flipped the page on my yardage book to get ready for the next hole. He looked back at me and asked, 'How many yards do we have behind that pin?' I glanced down really quickly at the page and answered, '10.' He wanted to hit it behind the pin and draw it back to the hole. Well, it was only seven—it was a big difference. We had to have a talk after that.

"Several guys have shanked balls really badly, but not many have shanked balls twice in a row. Bart Bryant did. He tried to chip it onto the green, but he shanked it so badly that the ball just missed me. Then he walked over and shanked it again. As he was getting ready for his third one, as a bit of a joke, I moved way back. Fortunately, that one managed to get onto the green."

—BOB "MR. CLEAN" CHENEY

I've seen a lot of bad shots over the years. I saw Lenny Mattice shank a 5 iron out of bounds on a par-3 when he wasn't even under pressure. That was a really bad shot. Hitting the ball right out of bounds on a par-3? That's not good for a professional golfer. I've also seen a number of 4-putts, and even worse, a few 5-putts—and a bunch of shanks. But the worst shot I ever saw has to be the one I hit. It was the famous caddie shot at TPC on the island green that happens every year on the Wednesday [before the tournament]. I was teeing off at 17 and I decided to go with an 8 iron. It seemed like a good club choice at the time, and as I walked up to the ball I was feeling pretty good. Well, I mis-hit the ball so badly that it hit the wooden plank holding the netting down right in front of me. The ball went straight up in the air and just a little to the right. Glen Day caught it in the air as he was walking off the 16th green and tossed it back to me. That's easily the worst shot I ever saw."

—JOEY DAMIANO

I try to block out the bad shots, but I do remember seeing Fuzzy Zoeller hit out of the bunker on a rainy day to put it three inches from the hole. Usually guys take their time and clean the ball off before their putt, but Fuzzy said he'd just finish. So he grabbed his putter and walked up to his ball to tap it in but there was a grain of sand on it. His putt shot straight off to the side and didn't come close to going in. Then he wiped his putter and the ball off and tapped it in."

—"MINNESOTA" MIKE LEALOS

I was working for Gene Sauers and we were leading in New Orleans after the first round. Then it rained for three days and we didn't come back out until Sunday morning. On the first hole of the day at number 10, he lined up a little right on the tee and hooked it left like I've never seen before. **Splash! Straight into the water.** It was unbelievable and he made double bogey. We went from first round leader to missing the cut. I walked ahead of him for the next five holes."

—JEFF "SKILLET" WILLET

I think the worst shot I've ever seen was Jean Van der Velde at the British Open. He had a chance to win—and he really should have won—but he made a series of really bad decisions and had very poor shot execution. He had a 3-shot lead, standing on 18 at the British Open. He could have used an iron off the tee to play it safe, but he hit a driver and he got away with it. There's a ditch in front of the green, so he could have just hit a 9 iron to pull up in front of the ditch, but instead he pulled out a 4 iron to go for the green and he ended up hitting the bleachers. **From there it just turned into an absolute nightmare.** At one point he tried to hit the ball while standing in water. It was the worst hole I'd ever seen anybody play. It was the worst-caddied hole I'd ever seen anybody play. I think his caddie must have been on Valium, because there's no way that anybody would let their player do what he did. He had a 3-shot lead on the 18th hole on the last day of the British Open and instead of walking up to the podium to accept the championship trophy, he blows his seemingly insurmountable lead and ends up losing it all in a playoff."

—MARK CHANEY

I was working for Ian Leggatt at the Canadian Open at Glen Abbey. We were on the 9th hole, which is a forecaddie hole. We were missing the cut and it was the last hole of the tournament. I was half way down the fairway waiting for his tee shot. Ian hit it but I never saw the ball. I asked the marshals if they'd seen it but nobody saw where the ball went. All of a sudden I saw Ian standing on the tee waving me back. So I started walking back with a new ball because I figured he'd hit one out of bounds. When I got within earshot he yelled, 'Bring the bag!' So I went back and got the bag and once again walked back to the tee. When I got there I realized that he'd absolutely cold topped the ball and it had rolled maybe 50 yards into the rough in front of the tee box—which probably explains why nobody saw it."

—GRAEME COURTS

I saw Tommy Armour III shank one on the seventh hole in San Diego. He wasn't playing particularly well that week and he just dead shanked this one right into the canyon. There was a whole lot of silence after that."

—DALE MCELYEA

Honestly, the worst shot I've ever seen a Tour player hit was by Carl Pettersson. At the time, Carl was playing great golf. We'd made 12 cuts in a row but we were right near the cut number on a Friday at the Bob Hope Desert Classic. We were on the 16th hole at Bermuda Dunes and Carl had just smoked his drive about 330 yards down the fairway. His next shot was a full gap wedge. He played it off his back foot and cold shanked it, straight right. It was a dead shank, an amateur shank. The ball was going directly out of bounds, and with it, his chances of making the cut. There are a row of condos off to the right of the 16th fairway. The ball hit the wall of one of the condos and kicked straight left, dead under a tree. He left himself with an impossible shot. There was an amateur playing in our group and he was shocked. He had no idea how to react to seeing a Tour player make a shot like that. Carl looked over at me and we both just burst out laughing. What else could we do? Anyhow, he went up to his ball under this dead tree and somehow hit it on the green about three feet from the pin and saved his par. Just like that, it went from the worst shot to one of the best."

—TOM ANDERSON

I was working for Joe Daley one week and we were between a 5 and a 6 iron. I lobbied hard for the 5 but he went with the 6 anyway. He stepped up and shanked it so bad it went two fairways over. He threw the club down, looked at me and said, 'I knew that was the wrong club.' He was too embarrassed to go over to his ball so he just hit again, this time with the 5, and put it within five feet of the hole."

—"ALASKAN" DAVE PATTERSON

"We were playing out west in a Monday qualifier and this player was looking a little nervous. He got over his putt, **then he backed away, heaved a couple times, and blew cookies all over the green.** I looked over at his caddie and asked, 'Who gets to clean that up?' I was happy I had nothing to do with that guy."

—ANTHONY WILDS

"I was caddying up at Poppy Hill for Jeff Brehaut. The ninth hole is a par-5 and as I walked off the 8th green, he grabbed something out of the bag. I assumed he'd grabbed his driver. It's a hole we always forecaddie, so off I went. So, I'm out there and I can't really see the tee box when suddenly I saw him coming up, waving his hand like crazy. Turns out he'd never grabbed the driver—he'd grabbed a bottle of water. The club was still in the bag. I had to run like a madman all the way back to the tee with the driver. Thankfully, he was cool about it. He's a real nice guy and nothing gets him flustered. A lot of guys would have ripped you up really badly. He just made fun of me for a while and that was it."

—BILLY CARLUCCI

"In 2003 at Olympia Fields during the U.S. Open, a girl ran out onto the golf course toward Jim Furyk. She had her top off and had some dot-com advertisement written on her chest and back. Judging by her looks she was clearly a professional. That shook things up a bit. What a great moment!"

—JOHN "CHIEF" GRIFFIN

I was caddying for T.C. Chen and he had a 5-shot lead with 13 holes to play in the U.S. Open at Oakland Hills, MI. It was one of the worst collapses of all time. On the 5th hole, he hit his ball into the high grass. He tried to hack his ball out and his club got stuck and he double-hit the ball. He made quadruple bogey on that hole and got a little rattled. Then, on the 71st hole, he 3-putted, which was almost impossible to do from where he was. Finally, from the bunker on the final hole, his ball rolled across the edge of the cup, lipped out and hung there on the back edge about ⅛ inch behind the hole. We ended up losing by one shot to Andy North."

—"MINNESOTA" MIKE LEALOS

In Florida one year my player shot a great first-round 68. By Friday afternoon, things had begun to change. On one hole she asked me what I thought she should hit. I said it was definitely an 8 iron. She hit the thing 20 yards short. She was obviously angry and yelled at me, 'That's the worst club I've ever been given!' I replied, 'That's the worst swing I've ever seen!'"

—BILL "JUNK MAN" JENKINS

I once saw President Ford hit a man standing off to the right of him. He swung his driver and shanked the ball. The guy tried to duck out of the way but it was too quick and too short of a distance. Wham! It hit him right in the side as he was diving to the ground. **Word spread quickly around**

the fans to watch out for President Ford and Tip O'Neill's group for the rest of the day."

—FRED BURNS

" I remember being on the 71st hole at the Canadian Open when I talked Fred [Couples] into using the seven iron. He really wanted to hit the eight but I managed to convince him. Well, he launched it over the green and one-hopped it into the back bunker. He made bogey on that hole, went on to birdie the last hole and lost the tournament by one stroke. He wasn't upset with me; we both just realized that I made a mistake. I always look back on that shot and think woulda, coulda, shoulda."

—JOE LACAVA

" I was working for Don Hammond on a Sunday and we were on the 15th hole at Hilton Head. It's a par-5 with a small lake in front of the green and a huge tree that protects the green. You need to hook it around the tree to get onto the green. We were paired with Tiger and after their drives both Donnie and Tiger were standing next to their balls with 3 irons in their hands. The difference was that Don was laying up and Tiger was going for the green. We both thought it was a little crazy, but when Tiger hit the ball it just kept going higher and higher. (You should have seen my face. I think my jaw was close to hitting the ground.) It carried the tree, landed on the green, and stopped within 15 feet. I'd never seen anything like it in my life. I just didn't think anyone was capable of doing that. After the shot Donnie looked up at me and said 'Artie, I'm in the wrong f—ing business.'"

—ARTIE GRANFIELD

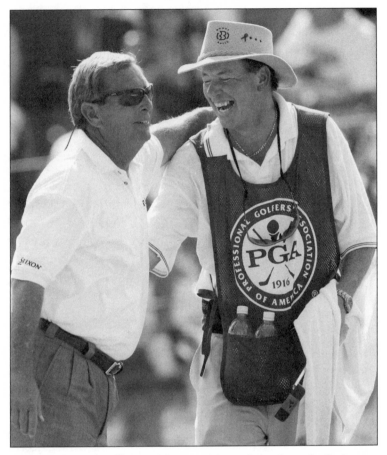

Fuzzy Zoeller and caddy Eric Schwarz celebrate their win at the Senior PGA Championship.

" Freddie Couples had just made a hole-in-one. Scott McCarron turned to him and said, 'Can you mark that for me?' as if he were going to follow up the exact same shot. He proceeded to knock it in, right on top of Fred's."

—BOB "MR. CLEAN" CHANEY

"I was with David Peoples and we were paired with a very young Phil Mickelson down the stretch on a Sunday. This was the year Phil won the Tucson tournament as an amateur. On his second shot on hole number five, Mickelson hit it over the green into a grass bunker with a 30-foot drop. The pin was cut right up against the bunker. When I looked down in there I could literally see the top of his head. I thought we had the tournament in the bag, figuring at best he was making bogey, more likely double, and Peoples was three feet away for birdie. Well that kid took a big ol' swat at that ball and it went straight up in the air and dropped down about a foot away from the hole. I've never seen a shot like that in my life. Mickelson went on to win by birdying the last four holes."

—ANTHONY WILDS

"The best shot I've ever seen was Steve Lowery's six iron shot on the 17th at the International for double eagle, though I shouldn't have been too surprised. We were in the same position eight years earlier when he eagled that same hole on his way to win the tournament. He hit it about three feet left of the hole, it spun right, and went straight in."

—DALE MCELYEA

"We were on the 18th hole at the 2004 Masters on the final day and Phil Mickelson had just birdied four of the previous six holes to tie with Ernie Els. At this point in his career, Phil had never won a major. He hit an 8 iron shot that left him 18 feet from the hole. I will never forget that putt. It went right in the goddamn hole. He's won some majors since, but that was easily the most memorable."

—JIM "BONES" MACKAY

" Tiger hit a 2 iron on the 11th hole at Memorial. It was a funky hole and everybody was laying up with a four iron, but not Tiger. Right before he hit it I remember thinking, *No way, not even he can do this.* Well, he hit it a mile high and 275 yards to put it a foot from the hole."

—"MINNESOTA" MIKE LEALOS

" The best shot I've ever seen in my life was at Westchester on the back of the 11th green where the pin was back right. We had absolutely no green to work with, and the ball was in this really thick hay. I don't know how he did it, but Brian Bateman just plopped it up, it barely hit the green, and went right in the hole."

—JEFF "SKILLET" WILLET

" I think the best shot that I've seen was when I was working for Jeff Sluman in San Diego. We came to nine, which was our finishing hole, and Jeff was not having a good week. He needed an eagle to just make the cut. It was a long par-5. After his tee shot he hit a 3 wood from about 265 over a trap and he stopped it about six feet from the hole. To be honest, Jeff wasn't just having a bad week, he was having a bad year. Nothing was going right. Then he hit this amazing shot to about six feet, went on to make the putt for eagle, made the cut, and completely turned his year around. He went on to win in Milwaukee and then headed to the Tour Championhip. For me, that was the shot that I'll always remember, because we were having such a bad time out on the course and he was just so miserable with his game. We were just trying to make cuts and we couldn't even do that. Then he hit this 3 wood out of nowhere. It just seemed to change everything. It gave him his confidence back and it freed him up to play the way he can.

Okay, maybe it wasn't the best shot that I've ever witnessed, but it's a shot I'll remember. It's the most important shot that I've ever seen. **It was a career-changing shot.**"

—MARK CHANEY

"There used to be $1 million for anybody that could hit a hole-in-one on the 17th hole on Sunday at Bay Hill. They'd put the pin just a couple of yards over the right bunker on a rock hard green from about 200 yards. There was no way a hole in one was possible. Lloyd's of London was insuring it. We weren't doing very well in the tournament and we were one of the first groups to come through early on Sunday. Don Pooley hit this low 4 iron, but it's headed right at the stick. I was saying, "Get down, get down!" It hit the top of the flag about five feet up, and dropped straight in the hole. There was one fan clapping. Nobody was around, but by the time we got to the 18th they'd come running from all over the golf course. It was packed—Don was shaking like a leaf and could hardly play the last hole. He got $500,000 and Arnold Palmer's Children's Hospital got the other $500,000. They never offered that contest again."

—RICK "RICK AT NITE" HIPPENSTIEL

"The best shot I've ever seen was when Hal Sutton was an amateur. We were playing some tournament down in Texas. He hit his ball off into the rough and the only spot that he could hit to get the ball directly on the green was through a fork in a tree. Not only did it have to go through that fork but then it had to draw about 20 yards to even get it near the pin. I was just concerned about his hitting the tree and knocking the ball backwards. As I took cover in case the ball would bounce back at us, Hal not only got it through the fork in the tree but he holed it. He hit a 6 iron through the tree and into the hole. That was easily the greatest shot I've ever seen."

—FRED BURNS

We were playing in the pro-am at Pebble Beach and I saw an amateur shank one into the ocean—but it was low tide, so it hit a rock, bounced back up on the green, and stopped about a foot from the hole for his birdie."

— JIM "SPRINGBOARD" SPRINGER

It was 1982, hole 16 at Indian Wells in Palm Springs. With his second shot, Gary Hallberg hit his ball left of the green. Unfortunately, there's a road that goes between the clubhouse and the parking area right there. So his ball hit the concrete on the road and it bounced up and landed on top of the roof of the clubhouse. It wasn't ruled out of bounds because that area wasn't marked. So he went into the clubhouse, through the kitchen, made his way onto the roof, and hit it back down onto the green. He went on to make the putt for par."

—ANTHONY WILDS

I was with Tim Petrovic in Illinois for a tournament a few years back. On the very long par-5 16th, Tim walked up to his second shot, which was lying in the fairway, and hit another driver shot. It was a really brave thing to do, and he put it about six inches from the hole. We still talk about that second driver shot today. I also saw Tim chili-dip a shot once. It went about three feet. That's a shot we don't talk about as much."

—RICHARD "JELLY" HANSBERRY

"I was working at the pro-am at the Bob Hope Classic one year and, sadly, I was working for an amateur because I didn't have a pro bag that weekend. The pro in our group was Carl Pettersson. The course is pretty easy down there in Palm Springs, the holes are short and on that particular day there was no wind. Carl shanked a 7 iron so bad that there was no doubt it was going way out of bounds. It was headed right for a house that really wasn't that close to the fairway. It hit the corner of a brick wall on the house and bounced all the way back onto the fairway. He managed to get it up and down to make par."

–CHRIS "CRISPY" JONES

"**In order to be a great shot it has to be a shot taken under pressure.** With this in mind, one of the best shots I've ever seen came, not surprisingly, from Tiger Woods. Actually there were two of them. They were during the same round and it happened on two par-5s at Memorial. It was on Sunday when the pressure is almost unbearable. Tiger launched these two 4 irons straight up into the air from about 240 yards to about four feet from the hole—one on the front nine, one on the back nine—to win the tournament. One of those shots alone was amazing, but to do it twice in the round was just incredible. Unfortunately, Stuart Appleby and I were paired with him, so it didn't end so well for us. Plus we made a seven on a par-3, so that kind of sealed our fate."

–JOEY DAMIANO

"I remember this one amazing shot by a fellow named Wayne McDonald. Wayne was a former Canadian amateur champion and I think he's tried the Senior Tour. I don't think he ever tried the regular tour—he was a stockbroker or something corporate like that. Wayne hit it intentionally fat with a 3 wood from about 170 yards over a 60-foot-tall poplar tree out of the rough. He called the shot and nobody even gave it a chance. It was certainly one of the greatest golf shots I've ever seen. He managed to clear the tree and he put the ball on the green. It was a very creative, gutsy shot, and what made it even better was that it was in a match play situation with the match even on the 16th hole at Wanaka Country Club in Buffalo. He ended up winning the match because of that shot.

"I also saw Sevy Ballesteros hit a fantastic shot on the 17th hole at Doral. He put his tee shot into a patch of rough at least four inches deep. The ball was not even visible from the gallery. It was about 130 yards from the green and he had to use all his strength to get it out. He somehow managed to hit it to within six feet from the pin and he went on to make birdie. I still can't believe he made that shot."

—CHUCK HART

I was with Rick Fehr at the U.S. Open at Oakland Hills on the 9th hole, which has water surrounding the front of the green and the pin sits dangerously close to the water. It was cold and rainy, the wind was blowing and his ball was lying in the rough. He hit a 4 iron at the pin and when it left the clubface I held my breath because I thought for sure that ball was bound to get wet. I was worrying for nothing. It turned out to be a fantastic shot. He managed to put it within four feet of the hole. At that moment, I thought that was the shot that would win him the U.S. Open. Well, he missed his four footer for birdie and Andy North made a 70-footer from the back of the green. From that point on the momentum shifted and Andy went on to win."

—HILTON "J.J." JAMES

❝I was working for Loren Roberts at the 2001 British Open and we were the fifth-to-last group coming in on Sunday. The grandstand was packed with people. As we were coming up the 17th hole he said to me, 'OK mate, we need two birdies to get back next year.' (The top 15 are exempt the following year.) His next shot was a 6 iron, and he put it to 10 feet and he holed that for birdie. On the 18th, he drove it in the rough and he put his second shot on the front edge of the green. The problem was the pin was 28 yards away to the right corner. Loren looked at me and said, 'Not what we wanted but it will just make it more fun when I hole that sucker.' I was holding the flag for him and he hit his putt from the fringe with perfect speed, as is always the case with Loren, and the ball curled straight down right into the center of the hole. The grandstand erupted."

—GRAEME COURTS

❝The best shot that I ever saw was from Mike Reid. It was an albatross at a par-5 at the Riviera Country Club in Pacific Palisades, California. It was the 1st hole, par-5 downhill back in the '80s. It was a Friday morning and we were one of the first groups off. I don't remember exactly the yardage we had, but he selected a four wood. Mike Reid's reputation with a four wood was lethal, absolutely lethal. He was well-respected. He hit it over the bunker and it took one or two bounces and went in the hole. **Walking off the green, I remember the scorer of the green calling in the score of the group: 'Five, five, two.' Then I heard her say, 'That's right, I said two.'**

"Mike Reid has a tremendous sense of humor. When he went in the pressroom after the round, they asked, 'What was going through your head? First hole of the day and you just made two on a par five.' He said, 'Well, when I got up on the 2nd hole, the only thought I had was trying to keep my drive out of the driving range.' That was back then. It's still true now, probably, that 10 under could win in the L.A. Open at Riviera. He had just knocked three strokes under par in one shot."

—CHUCK MOHR

I was with Seve Ballesteros at the TPC in Sawgrass. We were on the 9th hole par-5. He had a bunker shot with a three-foot lip to get over and it was downwind. He probably only had a variance of three to four inches to land the ball, and he almost sunk the shot leaving it six inches away from the hole. If you took 100 shots from there the closest you could possibly get would likely be 10 feet from the hole. After we were walking from the 9th green to the 10th tee, I told Seve that that was the best shot I'd ever seen, and in typical Seve fashion he casually replied, 'Some good, some bad.'"

—JERRY "SKYSCRAPER" SCHNEIDER

I was with Bill Glasson in Atlanta on cut day. We were on the 17th hole and he was in the trees but had a small space to get out and get it on the green. He said **'Jim, I'm going to hit this shot and we're either going home or staying for the weekend.'** Well, he put it a foot from the hole and went on to make birdie. We didn't go home. He made the cut on the number and by the end of the weekend had a top-10 finish."

—JIM "SPRINGBOARD" SPRINGER

My favorites can be boiled down to two great shots. One of the best shots that I ever saw was the one Steve Pate made at the International on Sunday. This was back in the day when if it was tied at the end of the day, you started over. On number 8, he holed a 2 iron for a double eagle. A double eagle is great no matter when, but this was definitely one of the best times ever for a double eagle because we were playing the Stableford system and this shot guaranteed victory for him.

"The other shot that is burned into my memory was at the Ryder Cup when I was working for Lanny Wadkins. He had had the match under control for most of the round, but the momentum had quickly swung the other way after a couple of poor shots. We were at the 14th hole which was a par-3, and if you didn't hit the green perfectly, the ball would roll off 20 or 30 yards away and you would be left with a really difficult chip. Our opponent had hit it on the green to about 30 feet, which was almost like a hole winner because the hole's so hard. Lanny hit his shot to 12 feet and made it for birdie to win the tournament. It was such a great shot because of both the wind and green conditions, not to mention the pressure of winning the Ryder Cup."

—AL MELAN

EIGHT

UNFORGETTABLE MOMENTS

CADDIE CREDO #8:
"Win or lose, caddying is the greatest job in the world."

My greatest Tour moment was at Spyglass Hill. At Pebble Beach you play three golf courses: Pebble Beach, Spyglass Hill, and Poppy Hill. Spyglass Hill is regarded in most circles as the toughest golf course on Tour. Dan was doing really well and, by the time we got to the last hole, we knew that a birdie would give him 64. He'd break the course record that had been held by Ben Hogan and Bobby Clampett since forever ago! His parents were there and the tension was high. So on 18 he hit the ball down the middle of the fairway. I started to consult my yardage book, figuring out his best strategy when he looked over to me. I asked him, "What do you think?" Meaning what did he think about what club to use. "I'll tell you what I think," he said calmly. "I think my father is going to watch me shoot the greatest round of golf in my life." He hit the next shot up perfectly on the green within about 10 feet and proceeded to make the putt, for his amazing 64. As soon as we got to the scoring tent, I saw Dan's parents. I gave Dan's golf ball to his mother and his father asked, "What were you two talking about on the fairway on that last hole?" Dan looked at his dad and said, "I told Greg that my dad was going to see me shoot the greatest round of golf in my life." That moment is up there with seven victories. It was a really special moment and I was so proud to be a part of it. That scorecard still hangs at Spyglass Hill.

We were on the 72nd hole at the Masters. Fred had a two-shot lead and he hit his drive into the fairway bunker. Normally, I am the most positive person in the world, but for some reason all I had going through my head were negative thoughts. After the drive, Fred turned to me and asked, 'Is it in the bunker?' I said yes. All I was thinking was that our best-case scenario was that he was now heading toward a playoff. Either way he was about to blow his lead. All this was going through my mind in a matter of three or four seconds and it was as if Fred could hear me, he looked at me and said, 'No problem.' Sure enough, he walked into that bunker and made the perfect shot onto the green. He went on to 2-putt and win the Masters, which was the only tournament he ever wanted to win. **That was 15 years ago and it sticks in my mind like it was yesterday.**"

—JOE LACAVA

I have been on the bag with Steve Lowery twice when we won tournaments, but my greatest thrill was a second-place finish. It was probably the most exciting finish to a weekend that anybody has ever seen in golf. We weren't even in the mix coming down the stretch and all of a sudden Steve makes an eagle and then a double eagle in the last four holes. Then, on the 18th, he had a 10-foot birdie putt to win but left it just behind the hole. **I've never been so happy to come in second.**"

—DALE MCELYEA

I've won big tournaments. I've had weekend checks well over $25,000. Of course those are fantastic, but **in my greatest moment, I didn't win a dime.** It was on Sunday of the 1999 Ryder Cup at Brookline when we came back to beat the Europeans. On Saturday night, we were seven matches down and nobody had ever come close to winning the Cup from that position. Our team held a meeting to figure out what we were going to do. Our captain, Ben Crenshaw, had to go to the press room to answer some questions and when he walked into our meeting it was like a jolt of electricity passed through the place. It was as though Jesus had just walked in. He was crying a little and he said to us, 'I believe in this. I have faith that something great is going to happen tomorrow.' When he said those words, there wasn't a dry eye in the place. It was unbelievable, the emotion in that room. We all just wanted to win so badly. After the meeting we filed out of there and headed back to our rooms for some much-needed rest to prepare for the following day.

"The next morning I walked down to join everyone in the lobby and it was like walking into another realm. Every single guy had his game face on. We went to the clubhouse, ate breakfast, and walked out to the course with fierce focus. As soon as the first tee shot went off, we could sense that there was a shift in the energy. It was frightening. It was unbelievable, really. We played out of our minds and after the first six matches we had them. On the board, every match had a U.S. flag next to it. The fans were going absolutely crazy and the European chant of 'Olé, Olé, Olé, Olé!' was fading as the Americans roared louder and louder. The victory that day was the greatest feeling I have ever had in my career. Beating Jack Nicklaus in the 1983 PGA Championship was a good feeling. Beating Tiger Woods at the TPC was a good feeling. But that Sunday at the Ryder Cup was easily the greatest feeling in my career."

—FRED BURNS

"   I won the Kemper Open with Tom Scherrer in 2000. He won $540,000 so I took home $54,000. Not bad for a week's work."

—JIM "SPRINGER" SPRINGBOARD

"   In 1990, I shared in winning the Kapalua International. My mother had passed away the week before and David Peoples was good friends with my family, so the whole week was very emotional. It was a great win with the best field in the world assembled and we dusted them all by five or six strokes. Coming down the stretch we decided to do the "nerd" high-five, but the television commentator didn't get the joke and he said that we completely missed hitting each other. I guess he'd never seen *Revenge of the Nerds*."

—ANTHONY WILDS

"   **Every time I walk off the 72nd hole at Augusta without being fired or embarrassing myself I think it's my greatest moment.** The Masters is my least favorite tournament of the year and as soon as Sunday is over, I feel like I've just come out of the ring with Mike Tyson. It's just such a hard place to play. It's both mentally and physically draining and it's the first major of the year, so everybody's all jacked up. I've been there about 12 times. That's 12 times too many, in my opinion. It's a great place to watch golf, but it's a tough place to play golf and to caddie. There's no other tournament that's tougher than the Masters."

—MARK CHANEY

"   My greatest moment on Tour was winning the 1997 Honda Classic. **I was down to my last $50 and I was**

running out of options. I hadn't worked the whole year and I was surviving by working the pro-ams and grabbing jobs as a spotter for the TV stations. The previous week I got a $200 check from CBS and I used it to pay for the taxi to the golf course. I even had to cash it at the Honda Tournament and tell the cab to wait so that I could pay the guy and get to work. Then, out of nowhere, Stuart Appleby won the tournament and it's just gotten better and better ever since."

—JOEY DAMIANO

I was working for Tom Purtzer on the big island in Hawaii. It was a Champions Tour event and we were warming up on the driving range on Thursday morning. There weren't many guys out there—it was pretty early—but **next to me was Gary Player, next to him was Arnold Palmer, and next to him was Jack Nicklaus.** Those three guys were hitting balls next to us, needling each other. I wasn't paying any attention to Tom and he probably couldn't blame me. I was hanging on every word coming out of those mouths."

—RICHARD MOTACKI

I was working for T.C. Chen when he won the L.A. Open. On the 6th hole par-3, he badly wanted to hit a 5 iron and I wouldn't let him. 'No,' I insisted, 'the 6 is plenty.' He said he really liked the 5, but I stuck to my guns and said no again. Finally, he gave in and hit the 6. He made a hole in one and went on to win the tournament."

—"MINNESOTA" MIKE LEALOS

My most memorable moment happened at a tournament in Denver. We were paired with Craig Stadler, whose longtime caddie is my buddy Jeff Dolf. The tournament was using the Stableford system where you get points based on how you're playing. For whatever reason, the last hole didn't matter that much and Stadler hit his approach shot about 20 to 25 feet to the hole. Once Dolf put the bag down and grabbed the putter Stadler said to him, 'Why don't you go ahead and putt it out?' Dolf didn't hesitate a moment. **He walked up to that 20-footer and drained it like he'd been doing it all his life.**"

—JEFF "BOO" BURRELL

I will never forget that Sunday afternoon in 1999 when we were playing for the Ryder Cup at Brookline. The American team that started the week wasn't supposed to lose. Unfortunately, by Saturday night we had such a bad deficit that we weren't even given a chance to win. I was working for Steve Pate and he had six wins on that final day. We had dug such a hole that we really weren't supposed to come back and win. On that Sunday, the golf course had morphed into a football stadium with all of the Boston fans rallying us like crazy. It was amazing."

—AL MELAN

My moment to remember would have to be the year when my family was able to share in two victories. My youngest son was at the Memorial and it was nice to be able to see him and make eye contact during the round. Then we won the Tour Championship in Atlanta. My other son lives there, and my wife flew up to see that win and share the excitement. **Golf is such a vagabond sport, you rarely get to share it with your family.** It was a great family year for me."

—BOB "MR. CLEAN" CHANEY

"My greatest moment out on the Tour had to be when I was caddying for Bruce Lietzke when he won the Senior Open in 2003. It was a big deal because he had quit playing both the regular Open and the British Open in the early '80s, even though he was exempt. He certainly wasn't expected to win the thing. His deal was that if his kids were out of school and on holidays then so was he. He just won't play in the summer. His family always comes first."

—BRIAN LIETZKE

"The biggest thrill of my career was when Mike Reid won the World Series of Golf in 1988—that was huge. Mostly because of the way things were set up at that time. Mike was an extremely accurate driver of the golf ball, but he was considered short off the tee. The World Series of Golf was at Firestone and it was a monster. It still is a monster. It rained all week, so the golf course played extremely long and somehow he still managed to win it. That was a tremendous feat on his part. And to beat Watson in a playoff—what a thrill! Back then Tom was the guy to beat."

—CHUCK MOHR

"The best thing about being on the Tour is that I go into every weekend thinking that my greatest memory might be about to happen."

—CHRIS "CRISPY" JONES

"When I first started out as a caddie I was on the Ladies Tour, so winning two majors with Julie Inkster in her rookie year was pretty cool. But I've also won on the Men's Tour with two guys who have never won with anybody else; I won with Mike Donald and I won with John Morris. I always tell people that anybody can ride a thoroughbred."

—DICK "THE ANGEL" MARTIN

The year was 1985 and I had just been fired by Chris Ferry. He was a strange bird so I wasn't too upset about it. The next week I was standing in the parking lot in Westchester, New York, when this little Volkswagen drives up, and out comes Rick Fehr. I knew Rick from playing in the mini-tours and none of the other caddies even knew that he was a golfer. I knew he wasn't a PGA member and he wasn't in the event so I asked him what he was doing there. He told me that he'd just earned an exemption. I told him I didn't have a bag, so he asked me to work for him. We finished 12th that week which was very respectable for a guy that showed up late in an old beat-up car. While walking up the 18th fairway he asked me if I'd like to work for him at the U.S. Open and I said sure. It rained the whole damn week and we just kept hanging around at –1 or –2. We were in fourth place heading into Sunday and played in the next-to-last group. It was so great being right there in the end, we were both nobodies but in contention for the U.S. Open. We ended up dropping four spots, but the players that passed us that day were Norman, Wadkins and Watson. Those aren't bad names to be passed by."

—HILTON "J.J." JAMES

We were standing on 18th hole on the last day in Boston and we were tied for the lead. This was back in 1989 and the weather was so horrible all week, we'd be out there from 6:00 AM to 6:00 PM trying to get holes played. Blaine McCallister just kept creeping up the leader board and suddenly there we were, down

Now this was a shot. Dan shot it out of the woods and into the hole for eagle. Unbelievable!

the stretch with a chance to win it all. I handed him the driver and walked ahead to the fairway as he prepared to tee off. In the pouring rain, he drove his ball perfectly, way up onto the fairway. I just kept walking past his ball and to the green. He was yelling at me to come back and bring him a club, **but I yelled back, 'No, you've got the right club, hit that!'** So he hit his second driver in a row, under amazing pressure, and he put it right on the green. He had to be the only guy that day to even attempt to go driver-driver on that hole, never mind doing it with the entire tournament in the balance. He went on to make birdie and won the whole damn thing."

—JOHN "CHIEF" GRIFFIN

My greatest moment would have had to be on the 18th green at Augusta with David Toms in 1998. I started with David in Memphis in '97. We won our third week together and we got to Augusta because of that win. He started Sunday's round at three over par and we were one shot in back of the top 24 at the start of the day. We were really trying to get into that top 24 because those are the guys that get an invitation back for the next year. He started off slowly, even par, birdied No. 8, parred on No. 9, and made the turn at one under. He played number 10, hit a great drive second shot, made about a 20-footer for birdie. Then he birdied 10 and parred 11. After he hit his tee shot on 11, he kissed his wife goodbye because she had to catch a flight. **He went on to play the most amazing golf I have ever seen.** He birdied 12, and on 13 he got a great drive around the corner. We had a yardage of about 197 yards. It struck perfectly. I was begging him, 'Let's hit 3 iron! Let's hit 3 iron!' He asked why and I said, 'Because we can play it long.' He said, 'Now, isn't it a perfect 4 iron?' I said, 'Yes it is.' He said, 'Then let's hit 4 iron.' Here's what I was thinking: if you mis-hit it one iota, it's not going to get over the creek there, so that's why I wanted to play it long. I backed away and didn't say another word. He hit it perfectly. It carried Ray's Creek one yard onto the green, rolled past the hole about 30 feet, and he two-putted for birdie. As we were walking onto the green, we heard this tremendous roar and we knew it was from Jack Nicklaus. You just know. His roar is distinctive—the loudest and the longest. This was his last hurrah and it would end up being his highest finish of '98. At that moment Jack was well ahead of us. David asked, 'What is Nicklaus doing now?' I said, 'I don't know, but we need to tend to our own garden. Don't worry about him.' So we went on.

"He birdied on 14. We'd learned a lesson on that hole. We'd made a double bogey there on Saturday from hitting too little of a club and it funneled all the way down to the right-hand side of the green where he 4-putted and made double. We had an in-between yardage on that hole, which in my experience it seems you always do because you're trying to get over that hump. It was a really tedious second shot because of that hump. David hit it just past the hole about 15 feet and had it just outside the right edge. He rolled it in. Now he had birdied 10, 12, 13, and 14 and I was starting to get really nervous. He hit a great drive on 15. He's got either a 3 iron to try and get it over the water or a 5 wood. We settled on the 5 wood because obviously long was better than short. He almost made it. When the ball was in the air, all I could think of was his winning the Masters because of this amazing shot. I had goosebumps. This ball was going in the hole. It was going in the hole for a double eagle and it was my first time there. I've dreamed about this situation for years and years and years. I've watched this tournament religiously, never missed it. His ball landed just short of the hole, and then grazed the edge of the hole. So he had an easy little chip and he chipped it up there to about 18 inches to a foot. I didn't even bother to go up there and help him read that putt because it was too close. He tapped that in and we went to 16. He hit a 5 iron, just eight, 10 feet right of the hole—a great shot.

"With every hole, we were moving up. It was like a dream you don't want to wake up from. I remember getting to 16 and seeing David's name on the big huge leader board, two or three shots out of the lead with three holes to play. This putt on 16, even though it was only an eight footer or so, seemed impossible. David literally had to have his back to the hole because of the way the green broke. We had to pick out something on the ground for him to aim at. To tell you the honest truth, I was praying, 'Lord, I need some help. There is no way I can read this putt. You've got to give him something out here we can point at.' I'm looking and looking and I see a spike mark sticking up like a Christmas tree—it was huge. I kept on looking and the more I looked, the more I realized that if it just went right around that spike mark it might have a chance. When we got back to the ball, David said, "What do you got?" I told him to go right around the spike mark, and that if he did that, it had a chance. The shot was perfect, and the ball tumbled right in the mouth of the hole. Now he'd made five birdies in a row. He was already six under par on the back side. I'm thinking that we have to be tying some kind of record. We go to 17 and he hits a little pitching wedge in there about 30 feet to the left of the hole. I'm reading the putt—same thing, "Where's it at, Lord? Show me something. Where's that spot on the green where we can go over so that the ball goes into the hole?" Well, no more had that thought just run through my head than I'm walking from the ball toward the cup and I see a ball mark right on the ridge that bisects that green. I knew that was it. I turned around, walked back to the ball, and waited for David to get back. He said, 'What do you got?' and I said, 'David, it's that ball mark there, right on the ridge.' He hit it right over the ball mark and the ball went right in the hole for the seventh birdie on the backside. Now I'm really starting to get excited. I'm double-fist-pumping up in the air and people are just running at you because he's making all these birdies. People are coming at you from everywhere, just rushing towards you trying to get in a position to watch him play the last hole.

"So as we walk off the 17th green, a crazy thought came into my head to smoke a cigarette. So I put this cigarette in my mouth and I'm trying to get the lighter. First I couldn't get the lighter to light, then after I got it to light, I couldn't get it to the end of the cigarette, because I was so nervous, my hands were shaking. It seems like this went on for a minute or two, but in reality it was probably only 10 or 15 seconds. Everything was so magnified. Because I couldn't get it to light normally and I was a little bit jittery, I said, 'To heck with this, I don't want anybody to see how nervous I am.' So I put the cigarette and the lighter away and we went on to the 18th tee. His tee shot went right into the bunker. When he got in there, he originally had 8 iron because of the lip. But the wind had just slightly shifted and it was up the hill and it was a questionable yardage as to whether the 8 iron would even cover the front bunker or the false front on that green. I called him back out and said, 'Let's go in and try to hit a 7 iron. Open it up a little bit.' The last thing I said was, 'Swing that club, David. Let that club get it out of the bunker.'

"Sure enough, he made a good swing. It was a tough shot to begin with, just to get it up around the green from where he was. He got it up there, pin high right, just off the green and we had the chip. He chipped it to about six feet. Now he was left with this six-footer for par, for 29 on the backside, 64 for the round. It was huge. Putts don't get much bigger than that. I made up my mind that I was going to get in front of him on this putt. He asked, 'What do you got?' and I said, 'David, what do you think?' He said, 'If I see it going any way, I see it going a little right.' I said, 'That's exactly what I see.' And it was. I was so relieved that we matched up. All I had to do was concur, just agree and try to get him the confidence he needed. He rolled that little puppy right in the middle of the hole. We hugged, shook hands, all that stuff. We went in the scores tent and I cried like a baby. It was so emotional for the first time at Augusta, to caddie and have a round like that on a Sunday—29 on the backside. I was reading all the putts like the Monday morning sports page. It was the last 29 that has been shot on the backside of Augusta and it might not ever be done again. **I've had wins on Tour, but as far as what I'll go to my grave remembering, it was the day we finished tied with Jack Nicklaus for sixth at Augusta."**

—KENNY BUTLER

I've had three wins on the Nike Tour and a second-place finish on the PGA Tour in Hartford one year, but my greatest moments and fondest memories have come from the times when I am working in the same group with the Growler or with the Piddler. Being around these guys is what caddying is all about."

—"REEFER" RAY REAVIS

In 1995, the media had dubbed Corey Pavin the best player never to win a major. Well, we wanted to change that. He was leading the U.S. Open and we were standing on the 72nd hole waiting to tee off. I just wanted him to hit it onto the fairway and everything would be fine. His tee shot was pretty bad, it went off the heel of his driver and he left himself with a very difficult second shot. We had 228 to the hole with the wind blowing right to left. He thought maybe a two iron would get him there. I argued for the 4 wood but I stressed to him that he really had to stay with the shot. If you ever see the replay of this shot you'll see that his hands are past his shoulders and his head is still down. He hit that 4 wood to five feet and went on to win the U.S. Open."

—ERIC SCHWARZ

"Things have always had a way of working out for me, but none better than back in 1993. I was getting ready to head back home to Australia to start a real job when I overheard a conversation on the driving range between Brad Faxon and his caddie. His caddie told him that he wasn't going to go with him to Sydney to work the Australian Open because he had a ski job. I told Brad that I was actually heading that way and I'd gladly work the Australian Open for him. He was in a bit of a bind so he said sure. Brad won the Australian Open that year and I earned a pretty decent paycheck."

—GRAEME COURTS

"I remember my first tournament back in '78 at the Bob Hope Classic. I was in the parking lot like everybody else trying to get a bag, when one of the older caddies starting messing with me and said, 'Hey you, you're green, you're wet behind the ears, you're not a real caddie.' 'What do you mean?' I asked. He looked at me and said, 'Look, you're not a real caddie until you've slept the night in a bunker.' For some reason, those words really made sense to me and **I desperately wanted to be a *real* caddie.** So sure enough, before my first year was out, I found myself in Hershey, Pennsylvania, spending the night in a bunker. I thought the sand would've been softer and more comfortable, but it wasn't. I soon found out that sleeping in a bunker doesn't make you a real caddy. It makes you a real gullible one."

—JERRY "SPEEDWAY" AIKIN

Not every caddie can say they've won a tournament, but in 1998 at Westchester I had my most amazing week in golf. I was with J.P. Hayes and we got every conceivable break in a 54-hole tournament. When it was raining outside, we were sitting in the locker room. When the weather was nice we were on the course. On the final day there was this unbelievable calm between us that I've never felt before or since. It was like some strange, spiritual thing. We did have to overcome some adversity, but we went on to win in a playoff. Unfortunately it was a pre-Tiger win, which means the paycheck wasn't as big as it could have been. But a win is a win, and it got J.P. into the Masters."

—JOHN "CADILLAC" CARPENTER

My whole career has been one big screwed up event, but I'll tell you what, even if I hit that lotto for $500 million tomorrow I'd still caddie. I just wouldn't be staying in these awful motels that I stay in now, but I'd still caddie."

—"REEFER" RAY REAVIS

I've been very lucky to have worked with some of the greatest players in the game of golf. I've looped for Craig Stadler, Buddy Gardner, Payne Stewart, Bruce Lietzke, Nick Price, and Ben Crenshaw (truly the definition of *gentleman* in the game). My first win on Tour was with Curtis Strange back in the early '80s at the Manufacturers Hanover Westchester Classic. It was the biggest of the tournaments at the time and it had a huge purse compared to other events. Curtis was able to beat Tom Watson and his take home check was a whopping $72,000. I'll never forget it. However, my greatest moment on Tour came in 1984 when I was working for Fred Couples. He was just a kid a couple years out of college and was making most of the cuts and playing okay. But at the Tournament Players Championship in April of that year Fred put together three solid rounds of golf and one amazing 64 on the Friday for a combined 11 under par and a first-place finish. Winning that tournament was everything to us. It got him a 10-year exemption on Tour (which is huge for young players) and a $144,000 payday. Even back then, Fred was great at staying cool under pressure."

—LINN "THE GROWLER" STRICKLER

July 15, 2008 was a date that I have had marked on my calendar for as long as I can remember. It was my greatest moment and I wasn't anywhere near a golf course. That was the day that Dan Forsman turned 50. For a caddie who has been fortunate enough to have enjoyed a long-term partnership with a great player, that player's 50th birthday is his passport to easy street. On July 15, 2008, Dan officially qualified to be part of the Champions Tour, also known as the Senior Tour. What other sport has a league for its older players where loads of money can still be made? The Champions Tour means never ever missing a cut. (The Senior Tour doesn't have a cut line except in the four majors; all events are three days, Friday to Sunday.) Not only does this mean guaranteed money every weekend, but it allows me to know my schedule. I no longer have to change my plans on a Friday because my player missed the cut. For the first time I know that I'll be in the hotel through Sunday and my roundtrip flight will bring me home on Sunday. Fuzzy Zoeller's caddie put it best when he said that caddying in the Senior Tour is the greatest gig in the world. It's a part-time job with full-time pay. It's my pension plan and it's something all caddies deserve at the end of their careers."

—GREG "PIDDLER" MARTIN

Conclusion

Golf, through the eyes of this caddie, is just like life, love, and business. 90 percent of the battle is just showing up.

We all live with imperfection. That is because we live in an imperfect world. Find a system that works for you. Even if it is not perfect, stick with it. If you hook the ball, play the hook. If you slice the ball, play the slice. Remember, an imperfect system worked consistently will always produce results.

If a baseball player hits .300, that means he gets out seven of every 10 times at bat. A good salesperson makes three sales for every 10 calls he or she makes. Most professional golfers make 80 percent of their "big money" in 20 percent of the events they play.

As with life, love, business—and yes, the game of golf—caddying is all about dedication. So make sure to show up, know when to shut up, and always keep up!

Acknowledgments

I would like to thank Dana Beck and her husband, Mike Harter, for all of their hard work and dedication. I would also like to thank the Toronto Blue Jays organization, especially Jared Gates, Janette Donaghue, Mike Neilsen, and Alex Tourles for their support and generosity.

My sincere thanks to all of the caddies who agreed to participate in this book; as well as Bob and Donna Schulz; Dale McElyea, president of the caddy association; and Bob Whitbread of caddybytes.com.

Thanks to everyone at Triumph Books who worked on this project, including Mitch Rogatz, Tom Bast, and Katy Sprinkel.

Thanks also to Dan Forsman, my boss and best friend.

And, last but not least, to my wife, and my love, Kathleen, thank you for your encouragement and support.